Table of Contents

Preface

I was born Jewish but grew up and studied in Colombia, a predominantly Catholic country. That's why I attended services at both temples and churches. While I was in medical training in the field in a little town called Pesca, I was taught how to baptize Christian babies when they died. Sure, it's unconventional for a Jewish doctor to baptize a baby. Still, under the cloud of death, I felt connected with God.

I was also involved in saving the lives of many babies who were teetering in the balance, and I came to believe that all religions played a part in the blessing of a tiny life spared. I witnessed many miracles in the neonatal units I attended for more than 42 years. Babies we expected to pass on somehow survived and experienced great quality of life.

> To me, religion is just an expression of your belief in God. All of those precious babies convinced me there is a God. They taught me to have love, respect, and appreciation for mankind. They taught me to have a positive mental attitude. They also taught me resilience and toughness as their struggle is like they're running ultramarathons throughout their lives.

I also developed a sense of family with all my coworkers. I became more understanding and tolerant of each of our shortcomings, often realizing that our faults are beyond our wishes and desires. That connection extended to the many families we interacted with day in and day out. I was so honored when they asked me to be at the delivery of their babies. I gladly attended, no matter the day or time, to celebrate their trust in me.

Toward the last few years of my career, the success of our neonatal intensive care unit (NICU) led us to launch the Tiny Baby Initiative. The intention was to deliver care to babies between 22 to 24 weeks gestation (5 months, 2 weeks to 6 months). This heightened my spirit and resolve even further as well as my love of all of those tiny miracles.

If life is like a movie, mine has been a blockbuster romance. I've been blessed with an amazing family, a career that fulfilled me beyond my wildest expectations, association with some extraordinary humans in medicine, sports, and other disciplines, and I've had a lot of fun along the way.

My heart is with those thousands of babies in my care who've grown up to make the world a better place. I'm blessed to have been able to help them spread their wings and live a beautiful life.

Gregor Alexander 2022

Tribute to a
Special Friendship

by Amy Saunders, daughter of Arnold and Winnie Palmer

Amy Saunders and her children with her parents, Arnold and Winnie Palmer

In 1965 my father, Arnold Palmer, came to the Bay Hill Club in Orlando, Florida, to play in a golf exhibition. It was then that he fell in love with the beauty of Central Florida and specifically Bay Hill's lakes and the golf course that surrounded them. Fast forward to the early 1980s: after deciding to make Bay Hill and the community of Orlando their home away from home in Latrobe, Pennsylvania, they were invited by a friend to tour Orlando Regional Hospital. It was during this visit that they were shown a specific floor within the hospital that was designated to care for children and newborns, some

Dr. Alexander with Arnold Palmer

critically ill and many born prematurely. This was the solely dedicated space for children and newborns, and it was woefully inadequate with minimal resources. It was then that they met a young and newly arrived doctor who had a passion and contagious enthusiasm, with a commitment to his work that seemed extraordinary.

While sharing the challenging circumstances and growing need to care for so many of the sickest children and babies in such a small facility and with a modest team, Dr. Gregor Alexander reflected on his view that most all would survive and thrive with a new, better-equipped hospital. Shortly after this visit and meeting Gregor, my parents were inspired to commit the "use" of their name, their own resources, and the exposure that would bring the community behind this effort. In addition to regional support, they quickly found how much exposure could be realized well beyond the state of Florida.

> Upon their first meeting and to this day, Gregor Alexander is one of the most inspiring and dedicated physicians you'll ever meet. I believe my parents wouldn't have had the same view and shared vision that compelled them to be so deeply involved over the course of many years had they not met Dr. Alexander.

Arnold and Winnie Palmer Hospitals

The exponential growth of a children's and baby hospital, with the remarkable team of pediatric physicians, nurses, and other medical experts that were recruited, was just the beginning. Gregor was instrumental in the vision and building of this medical center of excellence. It was a joint and collaborative effort, led by the hearts and minds of visionary medical specialists and those who sought this amazing care, which was acknowledged and rewarded by even greater and growing support. My parents, along with the many introduced or engaged, couldn't help but become involved after learning of or experiencing the extraordinary care led by Dr. Alexander. And just as many saw the greater potential that could be brought to bear under his leadership and expertise.

> Dr. Alexander was at the forefront when the Arnold Palmer Hospital for Children and Babies quickly outgrew a fairly new home, and it was clear that a dedicated facility was needed for children, but another facility was critical for women and babies. The relationship that grew between Gregor, his team, and my mother Winnie inspired the naming of the Winnie Palmer Hospital for Women and Babies, honoring her and the deeply committed efforts of support from an internal and external group of believers in the vision.

Gregor's connection to my parents was one of the most unique relationships that I have had the good fortune of observing and eventually becoming the steward of in my later years of personal involvement with the hospital. I have a greater appreciation for how and why Gregor had such a strong and powerful connection to people, but in this case, specifically to my father. They both came from humble beginnings but fought for something that was inspired by their passion and desire to make better lives — for themselves and, in the end, for so many others.

Gregor had a remarkable impact on so many, none greater than that of my mother and dad. He became one of the most revered "baby doctors" known, and each year at the Arnold Palmer Invitational, on the 18th green trophy presentation to the champion, Gregor's presence was as anticipated and appreciated as anyone else in attendance. What an amazing life he has lived, giving life to so many others!

Letter of Appreciation

By Annika Sorenstam, Hall of Fame Golf Professional

The most stressful moments in any mother's life are the hours just before and after she's given birth. So much is unknown and out of her control. Because of that, it can be rather scary. At the same time, bringing a new life into the world is an extremely powerful and, with the right doctor, remarkable experience.

> When I delivered our two children, we were thankful to be cared for by Dr. Alexander and his team. He is the most passionate and wonderful doctor I have ever met. We knew we were in good hands with him, as his love for babies and his ability to care for them are second to none.

We felt comfortable and welcomed immediately upon arrival. Dr. Alexander was available and approachable. Our questions and concerns were always responded to quickly and in a comforting, reassuring manner. Even our son Will's scary premature birth at 27 weeks went as well as it could. We called the team of round-the-clock nurses under his supervision "Our Angels."

Although our kids have now grown, we still remain in touch with Dr. Alexander. He lovingly checks in with our family and wants to know "how his babies are doing."

We will be forever grateful for his commitment to his patients and his profession.

Annika Sorenstam

Letter of Appreciation

By Maya Tharoo, NICU Graduate

Dr. Alexander with Maya Tharoo

Eighteen years ago, my mom was pregnant with me. I was expected to be born in September of 2004, but in June my mom arrived at her checkup before visiting her family in Toronto and was rushed to the Arnold Palmer Hospital to triage. At around 3 in the morning, she was told that she had to deliver me right then, at 28 weeks, by a young doctor who was not my mother's primary physician. They said that they had to try now, otherwise they could risk losing both of us. So, I was delivered by a team of physicians, including Dr. Gregor Alexander, on June 17, 2004 via a c-section, weighing 1 pound and 14 ounces, and was only 12 inches long.

For the first 40 days out of the 110 that I was in the hospital, my family was told that each day could be my last. I had to fight for my life each and every day, while my parents struggled with the prospect of losing their child. Although I don't remember the experience, it feels like I do because of the many stories the hospital staff and my family shared with me. What has always stuck with me is the support and care that my family received from Dr. Gregor and the hospital staff. As a result of those experiences and with the encouragement of Dr. Gregor, I started visiting the neonatal intensive care unit (NICU) monthly from the age of seven, where I shared my experiences from birth with families of preemies.

All of the families I've conversed with over the years have come from many different walks of life, yet we are immediately able to connect over our shared experiences with premature birth. I feel incredibly fortunate that my story is able to provide families with hope during their vulnerable times, and my experiences with them have instilled a desire within me to keep connecting with others.

Dr. Gregor remains my number one mentor and supporter as I grow and enter new stages of my life. Instead of supporting my physical growth and development as he did when I was an infant, he now supports my professional and personal growth as I journey through my undergraduate studies in hopes of becoming a neonatologist half as versed as he is. He inspires me to become a healer and have a full-circle moment where I provide care for preemie babies just as he cared for me. Beyond this, he remains a pillar of encouragement and an example of someone who has lived their life doing what they love. I have met countless families of NICU graduates who have children that were treated by Dr. Gregor during his time at the Arnold & Winnie Palmer Hospital. They have all raved about his dedication to his craft and his selfless approach to caring for their child. All of our lives have been bettered by Dr. Gregor's presence, and he continues to make lives better each and every day.

Letter of Appreciation

By Anthony Orsini, D.O., Physician, Author of *It's All in the Delivery – Improving Healthcare Starting with a Single Conversation,* Keynote Speaker and Apple Top 100 Podcaster

It has been said that If you enjoy what you do, you will never work a day in your life. I can say without hesitation that Dr. Gregor Alexander has never worked a day in his life. It has become cliché to say that someone was born to play football, born to sing, or even born to lead, but in Gregor's case it is no cliché. From early on, this man and this icon in medicine was truly born to heal. From his early years in Colombia traveling to his patients on horseback to his modern day building of a state-of-the-art Neonatal Intensive Care Unit, his life reads like a how-to book on the making of the perfect physician.

I met Gregor almost 10 years ago, when I had the privilege of joining him as a partner in his NICU in Orlando, Florida. I don't use the term "his" lightly, and although there were no ownership rights, the NICU that bore his name at the entrance was clearly his. And why not, it was Gregor's friendship with Arnold Palmer and his unyielding commitment to providing the very best care for the most critically ill newborns that convinced Arnold and Winnie Palmer to build the hospital that quickly became one of the largest and finest in the world.

For those who knew Gregor this was not a surprise. His dedication to perfection, his charisma, and ability to inspire ensured its success. His mantra of "Babies First" was the answer to every question, every problem, and every difficult decision. The "Gregor Culture" was the only culture: a calling to live by. The nurses and fellow doctors called him "The Captain" with reverence and respect. A title he deserved and carried with class and servant leadership.

In addition to neonatology, I have been teaching physicians and healthcare providers how to use compassionate communication to improve medicine through building relationships. I have learned many things from watching Gregor. He has the ability to form relationships and build trust with anyone he meets. I joke in my book that within five minutes of meeting Dr. Alexander, he will make you feel like part of his family. In neonatology, we treat the most critically ill babies, but their parents are our patients, too. Gregor never forgot that, always taking the time to comfort even in the worst times.

This book is a gift to anyone who wants to learn about a life worth living and what service is truly about. It is a must-read for those of us who strive to never work another day in our lives.

Chapter 1
Growing Up in Colombia

Cali, Colombia – 1952

The first five years of my life were like the South American version of the *Sound of Music*. My family lived in a large house in the foothills of the Farallones de Cali mountains in the West Andes of Colombia. Because Cali is near the equator, the weather was always warm and tropical year-round. The city was booming as the major economic center of the region, and it provided a good life for us. Green hills, palm trees, and seemingly endless rolling fields of flowers were a perfect playground for me and my sister Claudia, who was three years older.

My mother Manja spent her free time socializing at the country club, yet was always on hand when we needed her. Claudia and I played together and soaked up the carefree days of Cali's tropical weather. We had the privilege of a cook and a nanny who attended to our every need. Our friends and neighbors, the upper class of Cali, shared in the same luxuries we enjoyed. During the 1950s, Colombia had rampant poverty but also a wealthy segment. For me, every day was a new adventure that I looked forward to with anxious enthusiasm.

Gregor as a five-year-old with his sister Claudia and
mother Manja, shortly after his father left the family

Every few weeks, my father Heinz would take us on a family trip to
our farmhouse on the outskirts of Cali, where we had sheep, goats, and
chickens. My favorite thing there was the swimming pool. We would
invite our friends to the farm for a cool dip in the pool and, of course,
good food and drinks. On the surface, everything with the Alexander
family was perfect. As a youngster, I didn't know about my father's
relentless pursuit of other women. He was a habitual womanizer. I vividly
remember seeing one of his mistresses one afternoon. We were having
a festive party around the pool, and I wandered into the house. As I
opened the door, she was standing there totally naked. It's an image a
young boy does not forget.

My father was dashing, young, and wealthy, a trifecta that attracted a lot of women. The fact that he was married and had two young children didn't seem to dampen their enthusiasm. Of course, he was complicit in their advances. It takes two to tango, as they say. Or maybe the salsa is a better analogy. Cali is world-renowned as a hotbed of salsa dancing.

In addition to his appetite for women, my father was also extremely authoritative. Once, when my sister got an 80 percent out of 100 on a test, he warned her that for every point below 100, he would hit her with his belt. He made good on his threat one evening when she was six and I was only three. He removed his belt and went after her. Naturally, I wanted to protect my sister, whom I adored, so I ran to the pantry and got a broom. I figured I could beat him down and rescue her. I guess I had an excess of confidence for a child. As I was running upstairs on my mission, our housekeeper and my mother held me back to save me from the same fate.

Those were hurtful memories, but nothing compared to what was on the horizon. Everything changed shortly after my fifth birthday, when my father abruptly left us. He'd fallen in love with the mistress I'd seen at the farmhouse. He and his new lover were suddenly gone, moved to Chile. Worse yet, my father left us with nothing. We lost the house, the staff, the country club status, and had no reliable source of income. At such a young age I didn't know anything about money, love, passion, or betrayal. But those experiences made me grow up quickly.

In the 1950s, especially in Latin countries, women had very few rights, and men had the power to do just about whatever they pleased. When my father left, my mother was devastated emotionally. Still, she focused her entire life on raising us to be good people and to make a positive impact on the world.

As a testament to her incredible strength and resilience, my mother gritted her teeth and got a job to support us. That was early evidence that everything good about me came from her.

My mother found work through a friend of the family, who owned the Canada Dry Ginger Ale bottling plant in Cali. A spare room at the back of the factory became our home. I still vividly remember the deafening sound of the thousands of bottles rattling along the machinery. It was not an ideal place to live, but it was free, and my mother used her paycheck to feed and clothe us. Rent was not in our budget. For the first time in my life, I was experiencing poverty. That and my absent father left me confused and troubled. My happy, carefree life suddenly began to flow down a dark path.

My mother did her best to protect me. I remember crying often, and I became extremely insecure. Even though I was fragile, my mother had to work to put bread on the table, so she enrolled me in first grade. My teacher, Mrs. Paz, let me sit next to her desk so I would feel more comfortable, and I kept a notebook with me at all times that had the telephone numbers of all of my mother's friends. That book became my security blanket. During those early years, I lived with an overwhelming feeling of panic. I faked being sick many times so I wouldn't have to go to school, as I worried my mother might not be home when I returned from school.

Our cramped new living conditions inside the factory didn't help the situation, and the kids at school teased and bullied me because I didn't have a father at home. Divorce was a rare occurrence, and my classmates were mean and hurtful. It caused even greater anxiety, which led to frequent nightmares and bedwetting. Everything was going downhill.

Through some of my mother's connections, I was fortunate to attend a private Jewish school with support from the local synagogue. Attending a progressive school, along with the unconditional love of my dear mother, helped to get me through each day. However, I was still living an emotional roller coaster and my grades reflected that. I believe some of the teachers saw potential in me, but I didn't do the work needed to keep my grades up.

Still, life went on, and we soon had a routine. Mother would go to work, and Claudia and I attended school. Somehow we made ends meet, and our community of friends helped when we needed it. Even though she had every right to, my mother never denigrated my father. She still wanted us to have a relationship with him. Forgiveness was yet another of her endearing qualities. Day by day, we continued to move forward. Even without money, there was a lot of love and happiness in our family, although I still missed our cook's delicious food and nanny's care.

When I was seven, my life and my future began to take shape. At the time, I had a friend with whom I shared a strong connection. His mother had run away with another man, similar to my dad's disappearance. My friend invited me on a fishing trip with his father, and as we stood by the river looking out across the water, I had a sort of vision, like a religious experience. I remember it so clearly. Right there, standing barefoot on a smooth rock, I decided that I was going to be a doctor. I even knew what kind of medicine I wanted to practice. Even at that young age, I had an innate fondness for babies and children. So I decided I would be a pediatrician. It was like an inspiration from Heaven, and it just came to my heart and mind. I became absolutely committed to my future. When I got home and told my mother about my vision and what I wanted to do, she supported and encouraged me. "I know it's going to be hard," she said, "but don't worry, God will provide. Don't ever give up on your dreams."

Just when our lives seemed to be getting on track, more pain and misery hit. This time, the tragedy was out of our control. In the early hours of August 7, 1956, as my mother, sister, and I were sleeping, a massive explosion shook the building to its core. The walls cracked, and plaster from the ceiling fell on top of us. We knew about earthquakes and, at first, thought the ground was shaking. We later learned that a load of dynamite being carried on a convoy of army trucks had somehow ignited, destroying more than 40 blocks of the city and leaving a crater 150 feet wide and 75 feet deep. More than 1,300 people died that morning, and 4,000 were injured.

We were so lucky not to be among the dead. As we stumbled out of the rubble into the darkness of night, we were stepping over dead bodies and the dying. Horrible screams from the injured pierced the night, and the smell of gunpowder burned my nostrils. A cloud of dust rose into the night sky, and dirt was literally raining down on us. Blood ran down my leg from a large nail that had punctured my buttock, and my sister agonizingly pulled shards of glass from her bloody elbow. She was crying in pain. I was in shock, but my mother held tightly to my hand as we navigated the apocalyptic scene in our bare feet and pajamas. It took us a few hours to get out of the blast zone. I recall feeling a sense of relief as the gray light of the morning was glowing over the eastern mountains.

> "God was watching over us tonight," my mother told us. "He has a plan for each of us. Never forget that."

The event rocked Cali, literally and figuratively, but thankfully, medical and financial help poured in from across the country and the world. To this day, people in Colombia still talk about the explosion. In 1983, a movie called *Bloody Flesh* was made in Colombia, depicting that horrendous night.

As I think back, our survival that early morning was one of many miracles in my life. When my mother was seven months pregnant with me, she had an emergency appendectomy. An appendectomy was extremely risky in 1947, especially for a 39-year-old pregnant woman. It could have been why I was a little bit strange-looking when I was born. I was very puffy, and they speculated I had Down's Syndrome. By the time I was six months old, though, I was meeting all of the milestones of a healthy child. I was holding my head up and was starting to sit up on my own, so the concerns for me began to fade.

> Certainly, the pain and hardships early in my life shaped me into the man I became and fed my passion to care for the most vulnerable among us—babies fighting for their lives. That was my future, and I knew in my bones that I would be a caregiver. Of course, I never could have imagined how my life would turn out. I just held on to the faith and hope my mother instilled into me.

Not long after the explosion in Cali, when I was in the fourth grade, depression still had its grip on me. My grades were bad, and I was struggling to keep up. One day, out of the blue, I got called to the principal's office. I had no idea what I'd done or why he wanted to speak to me. Apparently, he thought I needed some tough love, and he reminded me that I was the man of the house. He told me I needed to shape up and take responsibility for the family because it was up to me to provide a nice life for my mother. That meeting was another epiphany for me. He opened my eyes and made me aware that I needed to stop obsessing about my father leaving. My mother needed me. That singular thought was all I needed to change my behavior. So from that day forward, I reframed my reality and started taking responsibility for my family.

Dr. Alexander,

From the first time I met you, you made me feel comfortable and valued. Though I haven't been at WPH long, I can see the effect you have on the staff, patients, and parents. You will be sorely missed!!!...

With deep respect,

Rebekah

A couple of years later, an opportunity arose for my mother to go to the United States for an executive job. We were still struggling in Colombia, so moving to Chicago and making some decent money sounded like a dream come true for all of us. We packed up our lives in tropical Cali and headed to America. Even though Cali was a large, thriving city, Chicago was overwhelming, but we liked the fast pace and the stunning waterfront along Lake Michigan. Yet, this was destined to be another difficult period. Once we arrived, my mother discovered her job came with one condition…one deal-breaking condition. The company wanted her to change her religion. We couldn't remain Jewish. Maybe in another era or under different circumstances she might have considered the change, but my mother had lost all of her family in the holocaust in Germany during World War II. There was no way she was going to abandon her religion. She refused to change, and the promising job was taken away. She was heartbroken but, again, showed her resilience and found a job in a factory making ice cream cones for minimum wage. From 6 a.m. until 8 p.m. she stood at a conveyor belt inspecting ice cream cones. If you have ever seen the episode from I Love Lucy where Lucille Ball and Ethel are working in the chocolate factory, that's kind of what my mother did. If you're unfamiliar with that television show, you should watch it for a good laugh. Only, for us, this was reality, not a comedy.

My mother worked more than 70 hours a week. We lived in a decrepit apartment, and my sister was placed with the first-graders because she spoke no English. For a 14-year-old teenager, that was terribly embarrassing. I was more tolerant, maybe because I had developed a passion for learning to speak English so I could help my family. Even though the whole experience in Chicago was traumatic, it forced me to grow up and act like a man.

After two hard months in the states, we decided to go back to Colombia, a more familiar country. Instead of Cali, however, we chose Bogota because my mother was offered a job at a Jewish temple and my father's sister, Aunt Marienne, lived there.

> The journcy to Bogota turned out to be a sort of fateful
> event because we missed our flight connection to
> Colombia at the Miami airport. There were only two weekly
> flights to Bogota, so we stayed in Miami for three days
> waiting for the next flight. We ended up touring the city,
> going to the beach, and taking in the lifestyle Miami offered.
> Little did I know that my life and career would eventually
> take shape in Florida, which has been my home for 45
> years.

In Bogota, our lives began to improve. My mother managed the Jewish temple and organized all of their events. We moved into the penthouse on the property, where we finally had nice living conditions and room to spread out a little bit. The temple had so many events, which kept my mother busy, but there were also many times when we were the only ones on the property. As I grew older, I would take the opportunity to go to the temple and pray alone. Being so solitary in prayer helped build my inner peace, and I grew stronger emotionally. The stability of a good home and caring community continued to be a good influence on me. I had my bar mitzvah and learned Hebrew at that temple. I started playing soccer at school and made many friends. After years of upheaval, I finally had structure and purpose.

Having my family living at the temple was also advantageous for our community. On Saturdays, the holiest day in the Jewish religion, we needed to have 10 men present for a quorum to have a service for readings of the Torah. They knew they could always count on me if another person was needed for the quorum. It made me feel good to contribute and be an important part of the temple.

At school, I became great friends with Luis, who was very tall and played on the soccer team with me. For some reason, we became like the good Samaritans of our class. Whenever there was bullying by someone toward us or another classmate, Luis and I would take the bully out of class and wrestle him to the ground. Then, all the classmates would gather around and sign their names on the bully's belly. The teachers didn't complain; in fact, they looked the other way, and it didn't take long before the bullying stopped. I'm not sure how we came up with that method of discipline, but it worked, and Luis and I continued to build a strong friendship.

In those days, most dogs that roamed the streets in Colombia were not vaccinated against rabies so any kind of dog bite carried a high risk of getting infected. One day, as Luis and I were outside the school, a wild dog suddenly ran over to attack a young student. It looked like the dog was on a mission. I was close enough to be able to jump between the dog and the boy and save him from being attacked. I guess my instincts to protect those in danger were already strong. Unfortunately, the dog bit me several times, and because we didn't know if it had rabies, I had to go through treatments just in case. Over the course of two weeks, I had to get 14 shots in the abdomen, which was very painful but necessary. Amazingly, as it turns out, that little boy I protected that day is now an ear, nose, and throat doctor in Orlando, where I live.

Like so many kids in Colombia, soccer became my passion. I played all of the time, primarily as goalie and defensive sweeper, which I guess is appropriate because Alexander means protector of mankind. Those who follow soccer know that the goalie has to be fearless; some would even say a little bit crazy. That's the way I played goalie and defense. When I was playing sweeper, I would either get the ball or the leg of the player—anything to stop the offensive attack. In the goal, I spent a lot of time in the dirt after diving for the ball. I still have a scar on my chin from hitting the ground after flying through the air to stop a shot. These days, certainly in the U.S., a kid playing youth soccer would have been rushed to the emergency room to get his chin stitched up. I just put whatever bandages we could find on my chin to stop the bleeding. We never even considered stitches. My mother told me the scar gave me character.

I lived and played soccer through high school and college and stayed in Bogota until I graduated from medical school. One classmate and teammate I became very close with was David Wasserman. He was even more of a soccer fanatic than I was. Every Sunday, we would get together and go to the hotel where the visiting professional team would be staying. We waited in the lobby, and when the players came through, we would get their autographs. Professional games happened every weekend, so the people at the hotel knew David and me. Of course, we had visions that one day we would play professionally and be able to travel all over the world. Perhaps, we could have advanced to that level if we had continued to work hard on our game. But my calling was medicine, and as much as I loved soccer, being a doctor was my biggest dream.

> That dream inspired me to study hard in high school. Unlike my poor grades as a youngster, I became one of the top students in my class and graduated high school at 16.

Chapter 2
Medical School

In Colombia, medical school was incorporated into college, so students could go directly from high school to medical school. I applied to a Jesuit medical school called Javeriana University. Out of more than 1,000 applicants, I was one of only 144 accepted, which made me and my family very proud. My first year of medical school began in January, so I was still just 16 when I started, but just barely. My birthday is on January 25th. After the first month in school, I turned 17. Starting first grade at five years old and going to med school at 16 is why I was able to graduate at 22. Not that it was easy. I had to work extremely hard. More than 50 percent of the students failed out by the second year, and only 56 of the original 144 of us graduated. The overall experience included one year of basic science and five years of medical school.

As if I wasn't nervous enough about the difficulty of the classes and so many of my classmates failing out, some teachers added to our stress by trying to instill fear in us. They were successful. For example, one teacher failed the entire class because none of us had our textbooks for the course. It wasn't fair to us because the faculty didn't even tell us what book to purchase. So, naturally, we didn't buy a book because we were all on a tight budget and didn't know what to buy. Then, on the first day of class, this teacher said, "You guys don't know the first chapter, so all of you fail." We all started the year with zeros, which was extremely discouraging. Our neuroscience teacher had a different way of driving fear into our group of potential future doctors. He said, "I don't know if I should fail all of you today or let society fail you in the future."

I know this was their way of using fear so we would have courage as doctors facing so much sickness, tragedy, and death. They constantly made it tough on us, and it worked. Looking back, I realize they knew what they were doing, and I'm thankful for their tough love.

Our second year of medical school was anatomy, where dissection was a significant element in our learning and development. We were to dissect cadavers, and we discovered just a week before our classes began that we get the bodies ourselves. Obviously, this is not like going to Walmart or even to a medical facility with a walk-in freezer to pick up a corpse. As far as we knew, there was no place in Bogota with freezers holding cadavers. We learned about a gentleman with a huge swimming pool filled with formaldehyde and many bodies floating in there. That was our golden opportunity, and even though we had to bribe him, we secured the body we needed. There were four of us in our group, and we pooled our money to buy a cadaver. Because my name is Alexander, I was first on the alphabetical list, so we were first to get the type of body we wanted. We paid him for a slender, 18-year-old girl because there was less fat, and the dissection would be easier than with an obese person. By the next week, the girl's body was on our table, ready for us to learn.

Initially, we all got sore throats and watery ears, and we were nauseous because of the overwhelming smell of formaldehyde in the room. Eventually, we all got used to the smell. We would even bring our lunches into the lab and eat in the same room with all of the cadavers.

> For the next six months, we dissected this young woman and learned a lot about anatomy. For the final exam, the instructors put a small string in a specific part of the body, and we would have to identify the nerves, muscles, and blood vessels and then explain their relationship with the rest of the body. There is no substitute for learning on a real body, and I have used that experience throughout my career.

Another aspect of anatomy, of course, was studying the bone structure. Again, we were challenged with finding human bones to practice. We couldn't use our cadaver because there was still so much tissue on the bones, and we needed clean bones. Fortunately, we could buy human bones from a man at the local cemetery. The whole thing was very mysterious because he wanted us to come at midnight under the cloak of darkness. According to the man, if a family did not claim a body after five years, he would exhume the corpse from the ground. Then, he would boil the bodies so the bones would get very clean. The entire experience was surreal, and riding home from the cemetery at 2 a.m. with a bag full of bones in the car was bizarre.

Thankfully, we had everything we needed: the large bones, like ribs and femurs, and the numerous and complex bones from the hands and feet, which provided the best examples to learn about anatomical connections.

As it turned out, what the man at the cemetery was doing was entirely legal. We also learned the reason he wanted us to come at midnight was that he didn't want to interfere with families who were visiting the graves of their loved ones during the day. Plus, he was busy working on the grounds of the cemetery in the daytime, so the nighttime business of selling old bones to medical students was his side job. It was still very eerie, but it was crucial to our success in the classroom that we got the bones we needed, no matter what it took to make it happen.

When I tell people this story, they usually don't believe me, but it was the only way to get what we needed for our classes. To succeed, we had to have those bones.

Our third year was devoted to pathology, and we did a lot of work on people who had been killed in accidents or had died at the university hospital. By the fourth year, we started wearing a white uniform every day, which instilled a lot of pride in us. We felt quite important wearing a lab coat around campus. There were many different majors, such as accounting, dentistry, architecture, and others, but we stood out among them all because of that white uniform. It made us start to believe that we were becoming real doctors, and we felt we were making our contribution to the world. It was a wonderful feeling but also a reality check when I was in the rotation and was called to see a patient. Wearing the coat doesn't make watching death any easier.

Our studies continued for the next two years with internal medicine, pediatrics, surgery, and obstetrics/gynecology (OBGYN). We knew after those two years that we had a year of medical work in the countryside of Colombia to complete before our diplomas could be signed.

Throughout medical school, I always had this feeling that I might have a learning disability, so I would get up at 4 a.m. every morning and study until classes started. For some reason, I had a hard time sitting still. On sunny days, I would walk around on the terrace overlooking Bogota to do my studying. Rainy days meant pacing inside. Of course, it rains there frequently so I would have to escape inside on many occasions. Those early morning sessions paid off. I studied hard and began to do so well that the head nurses noticed my progress. Most of them were nuns, and they were so pleased with me that they would sneak me into the kitchen and feed me in secret as long as I didn't tell my classmates. I guess being well fed also might have helped my grades. It was good for my happiness and well-being, and even though I felt somewhat guilty, I never told my friends about the extra food I was getting.

I ended up graduating number one in the class. When the medical school's dean called me into his office and told me of my ranking, he said I could choose any hospital in the country where I wanted to work. Of course, he asked me to stay there and work at San Ignacio Hospital, where the school was located. I did five years of medical school, one year at San Ignacio, and one year in the countryside. Then, I followed my dream of going back to the United States.

During my year at San Ignacio, my very first patient was a 40-year-old alcoholic. Amazingly, he had been drinking 40 beers every day in addition to some hard alcohol. Having studied internal medicine, and after hearing his story and examining him, I was not surprised that he was in liver failure and was comatose. Unfortunately, we were unable to save him. In all my years of being a doctor, I never encountered a more severe alcoholic.

> When my rotation took me into pediatrics, there was an area designated for newborns. I was fascinated and spent many extra hours trying to get these babies to pull through. That was a time full of joy working with babies and sadness when we lost one. I already knew that was the field I wanted to enter, so I was happy to put in the extra time to learn. Just being around all of those babies gave me a wonderful feeling, as it still does today.

Medical school was a tremendous amount of work, but we also knew how to have fun. Once a year, we celebrated at the school with a parade. There was dancing, drinking, and people generally just having a good time, and it was at one of those celebrations that I got drunk for the first time. In Colombia, we had a drink called aguardiente, which in English means very hot water. That was also an outstanding learning experience because I had a severe hangover the next day and decided not to get drunk anymore.

> I guess my life at medical school included a series of many "firsts." The first time I got drunk, the first time I bought bones from a cemetery, the first time I saw someone die, and it was the first time I had a relationship with a woman.

Latin America is well known for being a very romantic place. It's true, the passion of the Latin Americans is very real, and I learned about that first-hand during my medical school years. Five or six of my friends and I had girlfriends at the time, and at least once or twice a year, we would go with our guitars to the houses of our girlfriends and play some songs for them as a show of love and respect. During the serenade, the woman is not supposed to show her face, but can turn her bedroom light on so we know she's awake and we can sing to her. As it turned out, my girlfriend lived in a town called Cajica, the farthest city from school, so it would be the last place we would go. By the time we made it to her house, it would be three or four in the morning, but her father would invite us in. Two of the guys played the guitar and had beautiful voices. The rest of us tried to harmonize and sing back-up to them. It may have been that we'd had a few drinks, but I thought we sounded pretty good.

One time, we started a serenade, and a few girls came out to listen. They asked us who we were serenading, and it turned out that one of the guys had taken us to the wrong house and his girlfriend didn't live there. The girls were so disappointed that we weren't singing for them that they chased us off by throwing water balloons at us. We all thought it was hilarious, and we scrambled to leave but not before those balloons hit us.

I also had fun on the soccer field during medical school until we decided to have a game between the interns and residents. I was playing sweeper, and toward the end of the game, I tried to take the ball away from a guy doing his orthopedics residency. I slid into him, but he fell on top of me and injured my knee. When I went to the hospital, I couldn't move my right leg, so I called him—the same guy who hurt me—and he put a cast on my leg. I kept the cast on for the next three weeks. Luckily, my knee was fine, and I didn't need surgery.

Dr. "A"
9/23/2019

when I first met you Sept 19th 1977

I...admired you for being the "great Dr. Alexander"

I... then liked you

I... then respected you !!!

I... then loved you ♡

I... then admired you even more!

I... then felt and knew you were soo dedicated

I... then wanted and started learning from you

I... then knew I wanted to work with you for
 the rest of my life.

I... then saw you build "Alexander center of
 neonatology"

I... then watched you build your "Legacy"

I... then continued to watch your indefinate
 engagement to the NICU babies.

I... then watched families return to NICU
 asking for their "HERO"

I... then started giving you a "friendship kiss"
 on your left cheek every morning
 when I saw you at work ☺

I... then continued to watch your engagement
 grow stronger even After 42 years.

I... then watched you reflect on the
 word "Retirement" but **NOT YET** !!!!!!!

I... then Admired you even more ♡

35

Chapter 3
My German and Russian Heritage

While I grew up in Colombia, my family was deeply rooted in Germany and Russia, going back many generations. The tragic era of Hitler's reign clashed with the Alexander family, and they were able to escape. Millions of Jews in Germany were not so lucky and were sent to die in concentration camps. My grandparent's wealth and status opened a window, and they jumped through it safely, but they had to leave everything behind.

Maybe suffering was ingrained into my family's DNA. My grandfather, Chaim Gissin, was born in the city of Kharkiv in Western Russia. He was a Jew, a socialist, and a great journalist who fought ideologically against the dictatorship of Czar Nicholas II, whose monarchical rule in the early 1900s ravaged the lives of the citizens of Russia. The regime established by the Czar persecuted all Jews and young people with socialist ideals.

I don't know to what extent my grandfather can be considered a revolutionary. Still, I can't imagine a better revolutionary than one who had the power of the pen in his hands and the will to defeat an empire. In the early 20th century, my grandfather fought against the monarchist rule in Russia and for equal rights. He wrote articles against the Czar and actively supported the emergence of a government with socialist ideals, a regime later established by Lenin and succeeded by Karl Marx.

Because of his articles, my grandfather was intensely persecuted and sent to a prison in a very cold and isolated Siberia, in the middle of nowhere, where escape was practically impossible. When he was sent to Siberia, my grandfather was already married to my grandmother, Vera, who managed to go with him—not to the prison, but to the town where he was imprisoned. My grandfather somehow managed to escape to Germany in mid-1908 when the Czar had finally been dethroned during the outbreak of the Bolshevik Revolution. Ironically, Nicholas II and his royal family were exiled to Siberia after the revolution.

My grandparents escaped to Stuttgart, where they had some friends to take them. Safe in Germany, they had three children: my mother Manja, and my two uncles. Shortly after my mother's birth in 1910, my grandfather died of tuberculosis. Subsequently, my grandmother married my step-grandfather, from whom I inherited the name, Gregor. He was a man of excellent character who promptly took on the husband/parent role to my grandmother and her three children.

> The Alexanders were well-known and very successful shoemakers since at least the 17th century. We had a huge store in Stuttgart, aptly named the Alexander Shoe Store. The family was well off financially and socially, but after World War I, things began to change, and religion became our downfall.

My mother and father married in 1935 during the peak of the anti-Jewish movement by the Nazi government. Hitler was busy denigrating and marginalizing the Jewish population while building his massive military machine. He had become Chancellor in 1933, so the country was increasingly under his grip. Jews were persecuted in many ways—their businesses were boycotted, Jewish book burnings were common, and they were banned from civil service jobs such as being teachers and judges. The path ahead was bleak.

During this three-year period of my parent's marriage (1935–1938), the situation was becoming unbearable as the Nazis broke, burned, and closed all Jewish-owned stores. Despite the horror, there was a brief period during 1938 when Hitler granted passports to a handful of the wealthiest Jews from certain nationalities who were pre-selected by the Nazis. That is how my parents were able to escape to South America.

They left as quickly as possible with just the personal items they could carry. Traveling with my mother and father was my Aunt Marienne and my paternal grandparents, Sigmund and Betty Alexander. They were extremely fortunate to catch a boat from Hamburg bound for Cuba and then onto Panama.

My maternal grandmother Vera and her second husband, Gregor Gissin, did not have the same opportunity to leave. They encouraged my mother to leave, but they had to remain in Germany. Like millions of other Jews, they were sent to Auschwitz, where they were murdered in the gas chambers. Their son, my Uncle Max, was also taken to Auschwitz but avoided the gas chamber, most likely because he was young, strong, and a good worker. As the war dragged on and food supplies began running out, my uncle died from starvation just one month before the Russians liberated Auschwitz. Ultimately, my mother's entire family was lost to the Holocaust.

The fateful ocean voyage eventually made a stopover in Cuba, where they were met by General Batista. Apparently, Batista came to the docks and welcomed the refugees hoping to start their new lives in Cuba. Of course, this was before Castro and communism, so the azure waters, tropical green mountains, and freedom were enticing. Batista left power in 1944 after amassing a considerable amount of wealth but returned to the presidency in 1952—this time as a brutal dictator. Fidel Castro toppled Batista's regime in 1959 and brought communism to the island. Batista fled to Portugal, where he lived until his death in 1973.

It could be that my family had a premonition of Cuba's future, or maybe they just wanted to live in Central or South America. So they declined Batista's invitation to settle in Cuba and continued to Panama. When they arrived, my parents and grandparents continued to wander south to the picturesque port town of Buena Ventura, Colombia, along the Pacific Coast. Colombia was a long way from Germany—not just in distance but in almost every way. The ship's last stop was Buena Ventura, but my family decided to continue their search for a new place to settle. They traveled inland to Cali, where they found opportunities to make a living and, most importantly, there was no persecution from the government. My grandparents lived with them, but my grandmother Betty died before I was born, and my grandfather Sigmund died soon after my father left us. I remember Sigmund very well because he had a garage at our house where he made wallets and belts. I would spend hours watching him craft the raw leather into beautiful creations.

It took my parents three years in Cali to get back on their feet. My father was an excellent and charismatic businessman and started selling toys for children. My mother became a housewife and took care of the house and family while my father traveled the world on business. I can't say they lived happily during those years because my father always had extramarital affairs. He was a born salesman, and he became a wealthy man again.

Grandpa Sigmund was extremely upset when my father left us for the other woman. I'm sure the stress and embarrassment were harmful to his health. He died of a heart attack less than a year after my father left. The loss of both my father and then my grandfather was difficult and took a toll on my mental health for quite some time.

Chapter 4
Panama – The Reunion

I hadn't seen my father since he'd left 18 years before, but that was about to change. He was visiting my aunt and uncle in Panama, and they asked me to come to see him. I didn't want to go at first. It had been too many years and I had bottled up a lot of anger. My mother pushed me to make the journey to see him, so I eventually decided to go.

After his departure to Chile almost two decades before, my father had a tragedy of his own. His mistress died of a sudden heart attack at age 35, only six weeks after arriving there. My mother didn't tell me at the time, but I don't think I would have been sympathetic anyway because of how he had treated us.

He had gone south to Tierra del Fuego, Chile, to work for an oil company. He spent many years there, but he eventually returned to Germany to the small town of Saarbrucken. When I was in high school, he married a wonderful lady named Anne Marie. She was the one who encouraged my father to support me financially during the last years of my medical school.

Over the years, I had built up mountains of resentment towards him, but my mother, who had one of the kindest souls ever to grace this Earth, never spoke a cross word about him.

Gregor with his father Heinz and his Uncle Wolf

"He's your father, and you should have a relationship with him," she would tell me. "We are all sinners, and the Bible tells us to forgive one another."

My parents had stayed in touch through occasional letters and she encouraged me to meet with him. By the time I'd turned 23, I had experienced so much. I was a grown man. I had finished medical school in Colombia and was taking care of patients. I was also married with a young daughter, Lizette. I had overcome the obstacles and hardships he had caused, and I was finally living my dream.

So after all of those years of not seeing him and building up a million questions and emotions, I had the chance to reconnect with the man who had left deep scars on my psyche. To his credit, my father paid for my schooling for five years, so I was thankful for that. It didn't make up for what he had done to our family, but at least it was a step in the right direction.

As you can imagine, the reunion was very emotional. There was so much I wanted to say to him that day, like the pain I felt every day since he abandoned us. But with so much family around, I didn't have the opportunity. I returned to Colombia unfulfilled. While I was happy to reconnect with my father, there was still an emptiness inside of me, a feeling that I'd fallen short of any true reconciliation.

When I was well into my 40s, I visited him in Germany in Saarbrucken and we finally had a serious conversation about the past. I had just gone through my second divorce and was having a mild mid-life crisis, so it was good to spend one-on-one time with him. We spent a week together traveling around, enjoying ourselves, and talking. I think he felt guilty, but he never truly apologized, which was very disappointing to me. I attribute his lack of guilt to the fact that he was extremely self-centered. In business, he was the "closer" the company would send in to get the lucrative deals signed and wrapped up. He worked for a major pharmaceutical company called Rhone Poulenc in Paris. Based on the money he'd made, he was most certainly very good at that. He always drove a Mercedes. He smoked expensive cigars and was a member of an exclusive wine club in Paris. Someone had to die before they would take in a new member. He told me that to get into the club, potential members would participate in a blindfold wine tasting and would have to correctly identify the wine, year, region, and other specifics before they would be admitted.

He was very proud of that wine club and his business accomplishments, but none of that mattered to me. The only thing I wanted from him would not have cost him a penny. I didn't care about cars, fancy wines, or gifts he could buy. All I wanted was for him to say he was sorry for how much he had hurt me. But he never did that. Ultimately, the connection between us was never deep or complete. He didn't ask about my children or call or send birthday cards. It still hurts me today, despite the many years that have passed.

I also still have a hard time grasping his romantic relationships
He married two incredible women: my mother and Anne Marie, who
became like my second mother. Like my own mother, Anne Marie was
a wonderful woman. But my father did not learn from his mistakes and
continued to have extramarital affairs, even into his 70s.

After that trip to Europe, I visited him a few more times, and we
enjoyed each other's company. He died of Parkinson's disease in 1997
at the age of 84. I'd like to say that I cried, but I didn't. I'd done more
than my share of sobbing as a child. When he passed away, I was
mostly just sad that our relationship never grew into something healthy.

> Yet, being the optimistic person I am, I realized he had
> taught me a lot—mostly about who not to be. I learned
> how much value there is in compassion, empathy, and
> caring for the less fortunate and the sick and dying.

Those qualities are worth more to me than all of the riches in the
world. They cannot be bought. They must be earned. That's why I spent
my life filling my accounts with emotional equity and love for others. I
have learned that good things will come to you if you follow your dreams
and treat others with compassion. At least, that's how life has been for
me. The lifelong friendships I've made with the Palmer family, being
chosen to deliver Tiger Woods' and Annika Sorenstam's babies, saving
countless babies' lives. But I'm getting ahead of myself.

Chapter 5
A Year in the Countryside

After the emotionally draining trip to Panama that did little to fill the 18-year gap in the father-son relationship, I returned to Colombia to finish my one year of the "countryside experience." Medical school was not expensive there and was subsidized by the government because they needed doctors to go out into the country's rural areas to provide healthcare. They would only sign the medical diploma after that year in the countryside was complete. It sounded like a great hardship at the time, but to be honest, I enjoyed it so much. Most of it was on horseback because the terrain was extremely rugged, and traveling by car or truck was impossible. There were no roads in many places, only winding trails connecting primitive villages. I would dress like Clint Eastwood in a western movie with my cowboy hat and poncho and ride down a dusty trail. Instead of guns for killing, I had my medical bags and stethoscope for saving lives.

The local people knew from experience how rugged the landscape was, so when they brought me a horse to travel to a distant village, it was always very energetic and high-spirited. I had to become an excellent horseman very quickly; otherwise, I could never have made it over the steep mountain trails and across some strong rivers. Sometimes, I had to travel in the middle of the night, with only the stars and the moon as my guide, to deliver a baby or see a sick patient. I often had to travel all day and night because I was the only doctor in the entire region.

My base of operations was a small town called Pesca, the Spanish word for fishing. I managed a small, three-bed hospital with only one microscope and a nurse who, fortunately, was very experienced. I was still only 22 years old, but in Pesca, the three most important people in town were the mayor, the priest, and the doctor (me). The village was in the mountains of Colombia, where the year-round temperatures were in the low 40s to low 60s. Of course, everything was very primitive compared to today's standards. Very few people had electricity or hot water, and for a year, I took only cold showers. Even though I was receiving a small number of pesos from the government for my service, I was also paid with just about anything you can imagine—chickens, fish, vegetables, or whatever the family could scrape together. Once, someone wanted to pay me with a sheep. I had no idea what to do with a farm animal, and I definitely didn't have the time or expertise to take care of it. However, I decided to take the sheep and donate it to the town. This year was about learning, certainly not about getting rich.

I gained so much knowledge during that year, most importantly about listening to patients. I delivered hundreds of babies, primarily in the parents' houses. Because electricity was so scarce, I often delivered babies at night by candlelight. I can say that I witnessed a lot of miracles during that period of my life. I couldn't believe that the majority of extremely sick people survived. That year, I only lost a couple of patients out of the several thousand people I treated. Being so young and so inexperienced, I know that God was looking after me and my patients.

> It helped that the priest and I had become good friends. He even taught me how to baptize children in the Catholic tradition. On those few times when I lost a patient, I would perform a Baptism. I still do that to this day, and I believe God embraces those souls, even though I'm a Jewish doctor performing a Catholic service. I'm sure the Catholic church doesn't approve, but I believe God makes the decision to accept a soul when I commit them to Heaven in His name.

That year in the country, I also got experience performing minor surgeries. The customary payday in Pesca was Friday, and almost every Friday night, the police would come and wake me up and bring me people who had been in fights. The story was always the same. Someone would get drunk, and then they would fight. It was mostly family members. Uncles, nephews, and brothers would come in with cuts from a knife or machete, and I would stitch them up. On many occasions, the police would have to hold them down so I could sew up their wounds. The lacerations were not life threatening, at least not if I could stop the bleeding and close the cuts. It was great training, and I welcomed the practice, even though I got a little tired of the drunken behavior.

Pesca was the most incredible experience of my life, but I was on a path to the United States and the career of my dreams. I was leaving Colombia and going from the most primitive conditions to the most advanced medical facilities in the world. Was I ready? Not entirely, but I forged ahead, knowing God was on my side and I was surrounded by the best doctors and facilities in the world.

I also learned the incredible value of a microscope that year. I used it to analyze blood and urine and diagnose illnesses that way. That was a major step for the town, but the most impactful accomplishment of that year was building the town's first pharmacy in Pesca. Before I arrived, there was no pharmacy or safe place to keep the medicine and drugs they needed. Residents suffered from infections, parasites, and malnutrition. And because they didn't have vaccinations in that part of the country, there was an epidemic of measles in children with complications of pneumonia. Having a pharmacy was a significant medical advancement in Pesca, and I'm still proud of what we did there to help combat many of the medical issues they faced.

During my time there, I was treated with such respect and appreciation. The greatest reward was making a difference in the lives of people who didn't have access to medical care. It was a great privilege and, as I mentioned, there were many miracles. I specifically remember one woman who traveled from a very remote area. She had delivered her baby at home a week before and had contracted a blood infection because part of the placenta was still inside her. I was sure this poor young lady would die because her condition had progressed so far. All I could do was treat her with antibiotics and then hope and pray. Of course, I also had to remove the rest of the placenta. Amazingly, the antibiotics were very effective on her and she lived.

We only had two types of antibiotics, penicillin and kanamycin, which are both very common. Because most of the people in the region were never exposed to antibiotics, the bacterias were susceptible to the drugs, and the patients responded well to the treatments. That woman was a special patient, but truthfully, I remember every patient—including all 45,000 patients I've treated in Orlando. Every one of them impacted my life. I like to say that helping all of those wonderful people has made me an emotional billionaire.

My year in the countryside was a once-in-a-lifetime experience, but it was not without hardships. On my first day, I met with the doctor who preceded me. I wanted to get some advice: about the patients he was seeing, the villages, riding horses on rough terrain, transporting medical supplies—basically every aspect of the job. One subject we discussed was a powerful Brujo, a local medicine man, who had caused him trouble. For centuries, medicine was practiced by a respected villager who used herbs and rituals and the ancient ways. These were the healers—some call them witch doctors—who used homeopathic remedies on the sick and dying. Before certified doctors came on the scene, these Brujos were the only source of medicine available to remote areas. In my opinion, these healers were a necessary part of that society, and they did the best they could with the knowledge that had been passed down from generation to generation.

Unfortunately, the doctor I replaced had a poor relationship with this particular Brujo. He disparaged the healer and told patients not to see him. When a patient came from the Brujo for further treatment from the countryside doctor, he would be critical and tell them they should have come to him first. The nurse, who had been there for years, told me how the doctor had bad-mouthed the Brujo, and how the Brujo told the villagers to avoid the doctor. They had a bit of a battle going on, which, ultimately, was detrimental for everyone.

I wanted to develop a good relationship with the Brujo, so I didn't speak badly about him to the patients. I never said a cross word about him, and I especially didn't give the patients a hard time if they went to the Brujo first, because that was their tradition and they trusted him. That's all it took. Soon, the Brujo started sending patients to me if he was having trouble healing someone. I was always grateful to him, especially when he would get the patients to me before they were too sick. He realized I was accepting of his presence, and I embraced that he was doing his best. Toward the end of my year in the country, I got to meet this Brujo, and he was very grateful for my support.

Many doctors considered the Brujo to be a witch doctor, but I stood by the ethics of medicine, which meant not talking badly about your fellow doctors. Because the Brujo was a fellow doctor to me, I could not ethically criticize him for doing his best to heal people in the name of medicine.

I didn't realize it at the time, but a lot of what I learned from my relationship with the Brujo carried over with me into my career in Orlando. When a pediatrician sent us critical babies that they probably should have sent to the NICU earlier, I never criticized them or told them they waited too long. Even when pediatricians were beyond their capacity and over their heads, I was always grateful when they came to us for help.

> Every few months, our entire group—the doctor, dentist, priest, and nurse—would make a pilgrimage to remote areas for people who needed us. I was only 22, the priest was 23, and the dentist was in her early 20s. The nurse was the elder, but she was only in her 40s. We offered free medical, dental, and healing of the soul to very remote areas.

One time, at the end of the day, one of the very grateful villagers gave me a drink of chicha, a fermented beverage made from corn. They bury the concoction underground, and after it ferments, it tastes like licorice. However, it's not candy—it has more than 30 percent alcohol. Let me tell you something, I got very drunk and I developed an allergic reaction all over my body. I was stumbling through the middle of town, and people were wondering what was wrong with their doctor because they had never seen me drunk before. The allergic reaction was strange, but the nurse gave me a shot that fixed that problem. To this day, I don't know how I rode my horse back to Pesca without falling off. Of course, I was embarrassed about my behavior, but when people heard the story, they understood. They all knew the effects of chicha, mostly from their own experience.

During my year in Pesca, I took the medical test from the Education Council for Foreign Medical Graduates, commonly known as the ECFMG test. Even though I had limited knowledge of the English language, the test was in English. Somehow, I passed, which helped pave the way for me to come to the best country in the world.

2019

Dr A,

we miss you so already! I am so saddened by the news of your departure :(I want to personally thank you for all of the knowledge you have bestowed upon me/all of us over the years! The babies and families were not the only ones blessed to have you touch their lives with your compassion, kindness, and expertise! Thank you for being such an amazing human! You will not be forgotten I assure you. Your legacy will live on, I promise you that! Hopefully, we can continue to make lives better and keep saving babies the way you built this place to do! All my love and we will miss your smiling face here each and every day Dr. A!

Love,
Sarah

Chapter 6
The American Dream

After my Clint Eastwood adventures in Pesca, which taught me so much about interacting with people from all walks of life, I decided to follow my dream of returning to the United States. For a doctor, the U.S. was the crown jewel in medicine—home of the most advanced hospitals, best doctors, and research facilities. So, at age 24, after passing my medical exam, I applied to three hospitals. All three of my applications—Detroit, Baton Rouge, and Wouster (Massachusetts)—were accepted. It helped that there was a shortage of doctors at the time, so my opportunities were abundant.

I knew very little about America, only what I'd learned in Chicago during those two months we lived there more than 10 years earlier. I didn't know which hospital or town was the best fit for me, so I chose Detroit because some of my classmates in medical school from Colombia had gone there.

As I was preparing to leave my home country and embark on a new life adventure, I was asked to travel with a wealthy friend of our family. The old gentleman had survived several heart attacks and was in feeble health. His family bought us first-class tickets to Houston, where he had an appointment with Dr. Michael DeBakey, a pioneer in vascular and cardiac surgery. During the flight, the gentleman had two more minor heart attacks, but we were able to get him to the hospital in Houston still breathing. Unfortunately, there was nothing anyone could do, not even the amazing Dr. DeBakey, and our friend died a few days later in Houston. That was quite a way to begin my medical journey in the U.S., meeting perhaps the most famous doctor in the world and watching a family friend pass away.

I arrived in Detroit with very little knowledge of the English language and zero understanding of American culture, so I was initially intimidated. No one was at the airport to pick me up because they were so busy at the time. I called the hospital and got my new boss on the phone. He told me to take a cab to the donut shop. I replied. "What's a donut?" I could tell he was concerned that my English was limited if I didn't even know what a donut was. I actually had to ask the cab driver to come to the phone so he could find out where he was supposed to take me. Since then, I'm sure I've eaten hundreds of donuts. Even though they're quite unhealthy, I've learned that donuts are a great comfort food and a favorite in hospitals. Thankful parents often "surprise" us with a box of donuts, and they always manage to disappear.

Detroit turned out to be a wonderful experience. The moment I walked into St. John's Hospital and saw their brand new Neonatal Intensive Care Unit (NICU) and beautiful newborn babies, I had an epiphany. I knew this was what I had dreamed about since I was seven years old, and this was the career I wanted to pursue for the rest of my life. So, I immersed myself in learning everything, including English. They offered me free English classes, and eventually, I became a translator for the Spanish-speaking community.

The NICU at St. John's was built by my first mentor in the United States, a neonatologist formerly trained at the Hospital for Sick Children in Toronto. His name was Ali Rabbani, and he was Iranian. When I arrived in Detroit, there were 40 new interns, but I was the only one who wanted to follow neonatal medicine or neonatology. He was excited that at least one of us was interested, so he took me under his wing and mentored me for the next year. He tried to keep me in Detroit because they had built an exclusive children's hospital in that city, but I had already made a commitment to go to Miami.

The facility at St. John's Hospital was state-of-the-art because of Dr. George Gregory. In 1971, just a year or so before I arrived, he developed the first newborn respirator. They had a few of them at St. John's. This was the dawn of a new era of treating babies, and it completely changed everything. One of President John F. Kennedy's sons, Patrick, died of immature lungs. Yet, he probably would have survived if he had been born after Dr. Gregory's invention.

> I fit right in at the NICU. I was very proficient at starting intravenous fluids into the veins of these tiny humans because I had plenty of experience placing needles in shriveled veins of babies and children in Colombia. That year of horseback doctoring was paying off.

I had many other firsts in Detroit. I touched and played in fresh snow for the first time. People thought I was crazy just standing outside the hospital's emergency room, looking up and letting the snowflakes land on my face. I bought my first car—a Super Beetle Volkswagen—even though I barely knew how to drive. I learned about authentic American culture, like Thanksgiving and American football. Explaining everything about the turkey and cranberries and the big gatherings to my family back in Colombia was always entertaining.

Although I loved the snow, I think my body longed for a warmer climate. After a year in Detroit, I accepted a position in Miami at the Variety Children's Hospital, which was renamed Miami Children's Hospital. Now, it's the Nicklaus Children's Hospital, named for golfing legend Jack Nicklaus.

Chapter 7
Florida Bound

I'm pretty sure that growing up in Cali had conditioned my body to warm climates. I was enchanted by the snow in Detroit, but not so much that I wanted to spend my life there. The big city had provided a fantastic introduction to the American lifestyle, and my English had gotten quite a bit better. I felt much more confident about fitting into this new culture with so many opportunities and making my mark as a doctor. I'd heard so many wonderful stories about Florida, and I often thought about those three days we'd spent stranded in Miami waiting for a flight back to Bogota when I was 11. Even that short stay had made a lasting impression on me.

Fortunately, I was hired almost immediately by the Miami Children's Hospital. So, in true American fashion, I loaded up my car with my family and drove to Florida for my new position and life. I was so grateful to be in a place with some of the world's most advanced facilities. Sometimes, I would think back about my year riding horses to those remote villages in Colombia with little more than a stethoscope and a medical bag full of medications and minor surgical equipment to treat the villagers. Then, just a couple of years later, I was living in a modern, lively city and working in these ultra-modern facilities with so many talented people. Even at such a young age, my life had already taken many twists and turns. I learned to embrace new challenges, and, believe me, I would face more obstacles and miracles in the years to come.

Even though the Children's Hospital was state-of-the-art and had all kinds of specialties for children, including a pediatric intensive care unit, there was no neonatal intensive care unit (NICU). That was my passion— treating those babies who were the most vulnerable. But without a NICU, we would take our premature babies to Jackson Memorial at the University of Miami, where they had neonatologists on staff. Through my work at the Children's Hospital and many visits to Jackson Memorial, I got to know the head neonatologist at UM, a talented individual named Eduardo Bancalari.

Originally from Chile, Dr. Bancalari and I had a strong South American connection. We became fast friends because of our roots and our love of neonatology. He had established the NICU at Jackson Memorial Hospital and became a pioneer in newborn respiratory physiology. His process of managing respiratory failure in newborns remains the gold standard today, and his procedures have saved many young lives.

In one of our early conversations, I expressed my ultimate desire to become a neonatologist. Dr. Bancalari had seen the commitment and passion I had for these tiny babies, and he offered for me to spend a month at the University of Miami's NICU. I'd been in Miami for about a year, and I realized this was the perfect opportunity for me. To stay ahead, I worked my tail off every day. I had already experienced how hard work sometimes pays big dividends. This was another case when my efforts were rewarded. At the end of my rotation, Dr. Bancalari asked me to join the staff at the University of Miami, which I accepted.

As of 2022, this incredible doctor was still working at Jackson Memorial and performing miracles. During his years there, he authored or co-authored more than 300 papers focused on neonatal respiratory physiology, lung injury, and respiratory care. He's also received numerous awards both nationally and internationally. Perhaps the most prestigious was the Virginia Apgar Award from the American Academy of Pediatrics, which he received in 2003. Personally, I'm very proud of him for his work in Latin America, where he's made significant contributions to the improvement of neonatal care.

In addition to joining the staff with Dr. Bancalari, he offered me a fellowship once I had completed my pediatric residency. That began my career at the Jackson Memorial Hospital, which started out a little rocky. On my first day, I arrived early but had no idea where anything was. The resident who preceded me and had already completed his first year, gave me his beeper and pointed me toward the elevator to go to the delivery room and attend the birth of a critical baby. As I was going up, the elevator had mechanical problems and got stuck. It took at least an hour to get to the delivery room. Everyone was upset because I didn't show up on time on my very first day. Once I explained the story, they forgave me, but it was not a great way to start a new job.

Still, I was confident and motivated to do an exceptional job, so I'd get up early every morning to be the first to work. My primary goal was to ensure I knew every detail about every baby in the NICU. The nurses began to appreciate me because I always made myself available to them. Above all, I showered the babies with love and medical care.

> At Jackson Memorial, I was accepted to continue my residency in pediatrics. This became a bit of a roller coaster ride. I was supposed to be in my second year of residency, but they only had an opening for a first-year resident. I decided to repeat my first-year residency, knowing I would learn even more by doing so.

As fate would have it, the tables twisted yet again. Just one week into my "first year" I was told that a mistake had been made and one of the residents in his second year didn't have the correct credentials. Since I already had two and a half years experience—six months at San Ignacio after medical school, one year in Detroit, and one year at Miami Children's Hospital—they asked me to step into that position. So I basically went from a first-year resident to a second-year resident in two weeks. I needed two years (today it's three) to complete the residency but then, just six months into it, one of the neonatal fellows had to leave the country, which opened up the opportunity for me to do a fellowship in neonatology. In less than one year, I had quickly moved up the ladder. There was a bit of jealousy among my colleagues about my rapid rise, but it soon became a joke around the hospital. People would say that "the chairman of the pediatric department better look out, or Gregor will soon have his job."

I was fortunate to go from the bottom of the barrel to a fellow so quickly. Some of the residents who started their training with me were now working under me. It had the possibility of being awkward, but I just made sure I worked hard and put in the long hours so I could lead by example. I hoped I could earn their respect through my dedication.

My fellowship began in January 1975, just before I turned 28. The unit was extremely busy all the time, which I loved. For me, the constant activity fueled my passion. We sometimes worked for 36 hours straight without sleep, but I enjoyed every minute because I was part of something that was making a difference in others' lives. When we couldn't hold our eyes open anymore, we would sleep in the equipment room on top of the stretchers. If something urgent came up, the nurses would rush into the equipment room to wake us up.

Soon after I started working at Jackson, both my skills and nerves were tested. During one of my first newborn transports, I rode in the ambulance to Palm Beach to pick up a baby in respiratory distress. The baby was breathing spontaneously and needed to go to a NICU if he was going to survive. He had been admitted to one of the hospitals in the Palm Beach area, which was about an hour-long ride back to Miami. Once we retrieved the baby, I saw that he was having irregular and difficult breathing and that meant he could stop breathing at any moment.

After the first year of my fellowship, the mentors I was working for had to travel to Philadelphia to take their boards in neonatology. This was a new specialty and the first time anyone had taken those types of tests. Before they left, they called me into the office to tell me I would be in charge while they were out of town. Apparently, they had the trust and confidence that I would keep up the high quality of care that was needed. It was an extreme honor for a young doctor like me.

As I closely monitored the baby, I realized the trip was taking significantly longer than it should. Suddenly, I heard some loud profanity, which I will not repeat here, when the ambulance driver realized that he had made the wrong turn on the turnpike and was driving north toward Orlando instead south to Miami. About the time we realized his mistake, the baby stopped breathing. I told the ambulance driver to find somewhere to park immediately. The closest place he could find was a Burger King: he whipped into the parking lot as fast as possible with the lights flashing and siren blaring. For the first time in my career, I was faced with a situation where I had to perform an intubation (placing a breathing tube down the baby's trachea/windpipe). I had never done an intubation before, even in the hospital, because I had never had the opportunity. So, there we were in a Burger King parking lot, smelling of grilled burgers, trying to save a tiny life. I was able to get the tube successfully down the windpipe and get oxygen and breathing support to the baby. Obviously, I would have preferred to have been in the hospital with others to help, but that was not an option. Thankfully, this story had a happy ending: the baby survived, I performed my first intubation (in the back of an ambulance at a fast food joint, nonetheless), and the ambulance driver could breathe a sigh of relief that his mistake didn't cost the life of this precious child.

In addition to doing ambulance transfers, we also utilized helicopters for babies who were too far away. Although we didn't have a helipad, we used the Navy base next door. I have no idea how many times I rode in those helicopters, but I do vividly remember the wind whipping through the cabin because the doors were always open, and we were strapped in with only our seat belts. That was all that kept us from flying out of the door and plummeting to the ground. In emergency situations where we would have to land in the hospital parking lot, we would also have to be careful to avoid catastrophes like hitting power lines. Getting those babies to the hospital quickly and safely was our priority, and we did all we could to make that happen.

Dr. Alexander accompanying a critical baby in a helicopter transport

Some of the residents were understandably afraid of the chopper rides, but I had a great appreciation for it. Not only was it personally exhilarating, flying along with no doors and the wind blowing past, but just knowing that we were doing everything humanly possible to save a baby was enough for me. It also gave us a greater range of around 150 miles. We could go as far as Key West and down into the Everglades and farther north to the coastal communities.

> At Jackson Memorial, we had one of the first neonatal units in the state, and we used every means—ambulance and helicopter—to get the best possible care to those vulnerable babies.

Toward the end of my training, I was getting very excited about practicing neonatology on my own. Thus began the task of deciding where I would go. I believe America is a big country full of opportunities, so I applied to three very different locations: Dayton, Ohio; Albany, New York; and Orlando, Florida. I ended up getting offers from all three hospitals. Before making my final decision, I visited each location to tour the facilities, meet the staff, and get a general idea of what I could expect. Each position had its advantages, but I fell in love with Orlando because of the tremendous potential there. This was before Orlando had exploded into the tourist mecca that it is today. Disney World had only opened a few years earlier in 1971, but the evidence was clear that Orlando was going to grow rapidly. Also, the neonatal unit was brand new. (It was built in 1975, and I arrived in early 1977.) There were between 6–8 critical babies in the hospital and just one neonatologist. I saw so much opportunity to be in the middle of an adult hospital with no separate children's hospital facility.

During my interviews, I met with doctors and administrators, and I guess I was a little bit shaggy. In 1977, it was fashionable to have long hair, facial hair, and strange clothes. The styles were crazy back then. I admit, I did my part to fit in. I had a full beard and a lot of hair, and I looked more like a member of the Colombian drug cartel than a doctor. One of the interviewers was the first pediatric cardiologist in Central Florida. His name was Arthur Raptoulis. When he interviewed me, he joked that he didn't know whether to hire me or arrest me. He ended up hiring me, and we developed a solid friendship that has lasted more than 40 years. He turned out to be my best friend. I'm from Colombia, and he's of Greek heritage, and we shared a love of our profession and ended up working together for 42 years, nine months and seven days—a total of 15,550 days—to be exact. Not that I'm counting.

My very last day at Jackson Memorial was one I'll never forget. Instead of a quiet day where I could thank everyone graciously for their help and guidance, three sets of premature twins were admitted, so six little babies needed a lot of attention. The place was crazy, and if I could have managed it, I would have handled those babies all by myself, but we had to call in some other doctors to help. My soon-to-be former co-workers said that my last day at Jackson proved that a dark cloud followed me around. But I don't call it a dark cloud. I call it a celestial cloud because it's what makes me happy, and I'm blessed to have been able to care for all of these wonderful babies.

Orlando, Coming Home.

When I first got to Orlando in 1977, I was about to hit the big 3-0 in age. The overall atmosphere was reasonably calm. We were not too busy, but we had enough work to keep the two of us busy. Before I was hired, the neonatologist, who was from South Africa, was working alone. He had done a great job training the nurses and respiratory therapists to perform procedures that were usually done by neonatologists. Because he was all by himself, he needed the staff to be at the top of their game, which they were. He was a brilliant doctor, but I quickly learned he was quite difficult to work with. Many doctors are perfectionists, but he took it to extreme levels. Even when I did something to save a baby's life, it was never good enough. He was frequently critical of those of us who worked around him, which led to a lot of tension in the unit. He had trouble getting along with his peers, the administrators, and others.

Nonetheless, I gained a lot more professional experience and was able to practice all of the principles I'd learned during my training and fellowship. I was definitely developing my own style. Everything in medicine is about repetition so you'll be prepared for unusual circumstances. Even though it was a tense environment, I grew and matured from a professional and medical point of view. I was in my favorite zone—working with the most fragile babies—and the empathy I developed during that time grew exponentially. I realized what a great responsibility and honor it was to watch these vulnerable little humans not only survive but live productive and healthy lives. I learned humility, too, because not every baby made it. Life and death are part of the daily routine in hospitals, but that doesn't make dealing with tragedy any easier. Every one of those babies leaves an impact, the ones who survive and the ones who don't. I learned many valuable lessons with each of them, and I always conveyed to the parents that I gave everything I had to save their child. Sometimes it was out of our hands, and God called those precious children home. In almost every case, the parents were forever grateful for what we did, even if we couldn't save their baby.

> In my opinion, which may be biased, there's no other specialty in medicine that has the kind of impact on people that will last for the rest of their lives. I could fill another book with stories of the babies we saved who grew up to accomplish amazing things. I have included some of those stories in the final chapters of this book.

Even though I was learning so much and enjoying the time with the babies, as time wore on, I contemplated leaving my position for another hospital. The environment became too toxic for me to do my job. As all of those thoughts were swirling around in my mind, I made a trip to Baltimore to take my boards in pediatrics. While I was there and focused on the testing, I received a call from the hospital, letting me know they had asked my co-worker, the neonatologist from South Africa, to leave. They asked me to stay and assume the position of director of the NICU. That was music to my ears, and I was even more excited to go to work.

When I returned from Baltimore I realized that, even though he was difficult to work with, some of the staff had developed a strong loyalty to him. The last thing I wanted was for highly-trained and essential workers to quit. Replacing staff was always a chore, but I held a meeting and

Dr. Alexander and the staff of the NICU

asked each staff member to stay and give me a chance. I promised I would carry on the high quality of care they were used to, and I would treat them with kindness and respect. It must have worked, because no one left, and our team just kept getting stronger.

For the next two years, I worked non-stop. I was on-call 24/7 since I was now flying solo. The survival rate of our babies grew to more than 90%. I was working day and night and also meeting with a group of pediatricians and pediatric subspecialists about the need for a children's hospital in Orlando. The city was growing rapidly, and we wanted to keep up with the population explosion. Also, we didn't want to send our patients to other cities and facilities, or separate the babies from their parents and families. Our committee of nine doctors and one attorney began planting seeds of building a children's hospital. We did a feasibility study and presented the results to a medical system that is now called Orlando Health. They almost immediately embraced the idea of building a new hospital dedicated to children. Our neonatal unit was getting very busy, and I was traveling all over the city treating babies and transferring them to our NICU when beds were available.

The priority of building a hospital dedicated to children was becoming more and more urgent. This was the late 70s/ early 80s, and Disney's impact was spreading like ripples from a pebble dropped in a pond. Universal Studios was coming to town, and SeaWorld was building a massive amusement park. Orlando was developing into the children's capital of the world.

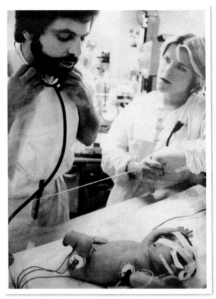

Dr. Alexander with NICU nurse and patient

At the time, our department only occupied part of a floor in the hospital. Because we didn't have enough facilities or the proper equipment, we weren't able to accommodate or care for a significant number of babies. We needed a hospital dedicated to babies and children that also connected to a hospital with a delivery room.

The crowding had gotten so bad that some of the sickest babies were being sent out of state to other facilities. At the time, around 1981, Bob Graham was governor of Florida and Ronald Reagan was president. Somehow, the president heard that babies were taken to other states and that Florida didn't have adequate facilities. Apparently, President Reagan called Governor Graham and told him that Florida needed to build more hospitals and also expand the capacity of the existing facilities to take care of these newborns. That gave us an added boost to not only convince ourselves but also the Orlando medical community that the situation was dire. We needed bigger facilities desperately.

During that time, our committee kept pursuing the goals of building the first children's hospital in Central Florida. The Orlando Hospital system had already embraced this vision, so it was a matter of raising money and implementing our plan. Orlando was booming, and those of us who lived and worked there could see what was coming.

Dear Dr A.

There is no way that I can express how grateful I am for your help and kindness. This card is just not big enough... Thank you for teaching me, thank you for encouraging me, thank you for making me laugh and thank you for sharing me how to love my job and have a purpose. I hope one day I will be as passionate and great at my job as you are.

Hope to see you soon!!

köszönöm ←(thank you in Hungarian)

Ruthie

Chapter 8
My Introduction to Golf Royalty

Arnold Palmer had moved to Orlando in the 1980s and had bought Bay Hill Golf Club. He began developing the area and founded the golf tournament that eventually was named after him, the Arnold Palmer Invitational. I believe it was a celestial gift to all of us that one of the hospital board members invited Mr. Palmer to visit our neonatal unit and pediatric floor, which were both located in the adult hospital. I remember the morning of Mr. Palmer's visit because I was notified that I would be giving the tour of the unit.

> I had no idea who Arnold Palmer was, nor did I have much interest in golf. I was given a quick background of Mr. Palmer's living legend status as a golfer. Fortunately, I'm a quick learner, and I immediately grasped the massive opportunity in front of us.

As he arrived, surrounded by a group of admiring administrators and board members, I met an individual who was very humble, warm, and charismatic. Despite his importance to the game of golf and the fame he had achieved around the entire world, he was incredibly genuine

Arnold Palmer

and focused on helping our community. The tour opened his eyes to the miracles we were making possible for tiny and high-risk babies in a crowded and constrained environment. At the time, we had between 20–25 babies in our small unit. He was so impressed that we could treat those babies in our little facility, and he was so touched by our vision for the children's hospital, he immediately supported us.

> "We can do better for our babies and children," he said. Those words, I will never forget.

That night, at a foundation event, he spoke passionately about what he had witnessed during the visit to our neonatal unit and the need for the building of the first children's hospital in Orlando. He agreed that the hospital could be named after him with a few conditions. First, the hospital would never smell like a hospital. Second, that our little patients would receive the most comprehensive, state-of-the-art medical care with tremendous caring and compassion. And third, no matter how busy and successful we became, every patient and family would be cared for as if they were the only one.

Based on the belief and support by Mr. Palmer, we were able to raise the funds needed for the building of a highly advanced facility within a few years. Because of his renowned reputation, he helped open many doors around the city and country and made our job that much easier. I was honored and gratified to be part of this historic and monumental undertaking while we continued finding creative ways to accommodate the ever-growing needs for babies and children.

Once we had the funds and approval to build the Arnold Palmer Hospital for Children and Babies, it was still going to be eight years before it was complete. We needed more space immediately, so I took the initiative to go to Advent Health (it was called Florida Hospital at the time) and asked if we could open a NICU for babies with a lower acuity at the adult hospital. Even though it was a competing hospital, the president of Advent Health approved the idea, so we opened the NICU there. That allowed us to keep "our" babies there and not have to send them to different cities. Once we opened the Arnold Palmer Hospital for Children and Babies, we were asked to leave Advent Health because we couldn't be in both places at once. Very few people remember that our group built that initial NICU facility.

Getting Partners

In Orlando, I grew the NICU steadily and began bringing in more partners. Ironically, one of my first partners was from South Africa. Based on my first experience with South African doctors, I was a bit worried, but this time was totally different. His name was Brian Lipman, and he was one of the kindest guys I'd ever met. He came to Orlando for one year as a chief pediatric resident and then went back to Duke for two years to do his fellowship in neonatology. When he finished his time at Duke, I hired him full time. I wanted to be sure to get partners who shared the same philosophy. He joined me in 1981, the same year I fatefully met Arnold Palmer.

Chapter 9

People to People International - China and Russia

While the hospital was being built, I stayed very involved in the process. However, I also had the opportunity to travel out of the country and do some very rewarding work. In fact, one of the highlights of my satisfying, four-decade-plus career was the opportunity to travel to China and Russia with People to People International (PPI), a nonprofit organization that promotes "peace through understanding."

PPI is a forward-thinking group founded by President Dwight D. Eisenhower in 1956. Their mission statement is to "enhance international understanding and friendship through educational, cultural, and humanitarian activities involving the exchange of ideas and experiences directly among peoples of different countries and diverse cultures." Eisenhower is quoted as saying, "A sense of humor is part of the art of leadership, of getting along with people, of getting things done." I've always agreed with that philosophy (about getting things done), so working with PPI was really a dream come true for me as well as the other professionals in our team.

My initial mission trip was to China in 1985. Our group of neonatologists, nurses, obstetricians, administrators, and pastors had been invited by the Chinese Medical Society, and I had the honor of being the representative for the hospital. We were able to tour several major cities—Hangzhou, Beijing and Shanghai—all the while under the close scrutiny and watchful eye of a Chinese government security agent who traveled with us everywhere as our "guide."

For me, the most amazing experience was seeing China before it had become industrialized as it is now. There were only a few cars on the road, but thousands upon thousands of bicycles, some carrying objects as large as refrigerators. Their ambition and innovation was clearly on display then, and we knew it was only a matter of time before China would be a major economic force in the world. Our official business was to visit hospitals and obstetric units and share our modern medical treatments and techniques with them. We accomplished those goals and also experienced and learned their methods. What really surprised me was that most of the anesthesia they administered was by acupuncture. It worked well in most cases, and that was a real eye-opener for those of us from the United States who were not used to homeopathic alternatives to drugs.

Using long, thin pins and finding the pressure points to block pain is a tradition they've used and perfected over thousands of years. We even witnessed a cesarean section birth using only acupuncture as the anesthesia and the patient showed no physical discomfort. Now, of course, acupuncture is available in the U.S. and worldwide, but back then, most medical professionals were skeptical.

Part of my contribution to the overall PPI cause, with the support of a translator, was to give lectures at the Beijing Medical School about a neonatal condition called Necrotizing Enterocolitis (NEC). This is a moderate to severe intestinal disorder that impacts mostly premature infants and, in severe cases, could lead to intestinal failure, bowel perforation, and eventual death. To this day, the condition is not well understood. While I knew the information I was presenting was beneficial, I also realized that translating from English to Chinese was quite lengthy, so I dramatically cut the presentation from an hour to about 15 minutes.

In addition to the collaborative work we did, we were also allowed to be tourists part of the time. We visited the tomb of their deceased leader, Mao Zedong, whose body was preserved and enclosed in a glass tomb. Thankfully, we were moved up to the front of the line because thousands of Chinese people had been waiting to see him since 2:00 am. We also toured the Great Wall of China and the Forbidden City, which were both as impressive as we expected.

We also had a fantastic tour of the Beijing Zoo where they had a huge population of panda bears. One oddity we noticed was that we didn't see any dogs running around in the streets or, for that matter, anywhere. We heard rumors that dogs were euthanized and served at meals. It made sense, although we never confirmed that to be true.

A couple of things happened that made us realize how insulated the Chinese people were from the rest of the world. One of the obstetricians was African American, and when we were in the Forbidden City, he was surrounded by people who had never seen a dark-skinned person before. Many of them came up to him and touched his skin thinking that it had been tinted and wasn't real. He was very accommodating and let a lot of people rub on him to satisfy their curiosity. Another incident was with one of our nurses who had very large breasts. Out of the blue, a Chinese monk reached out and squeezed her breasts to see if they were real. She was a good sport about it and didn't cause a scene. I did notice that the monk walked away with a big smile on his face. Seeing the reactions of the local people made me realize how fortunate we are to live in a country with a melting pot of cultures where we experience a wide variety of religions and races every day, and it becomes something we don't even think about.

We all considered the trip to be extremely successful. It took some prodding and a few drinks, but we found out on our last day that our "guide" was really a government employee sent to keep an eye on this group of unruly Americans. We learned as much about them as they did about us, and I believe that Eisenhower's goals were definitely realized.

Interestingly, five years before our trip, in 1980, China had implemented a law that limited families to just one child. The policy was controversial and was intended to slow their rapid population growth. We were all well aware of the one baby per family policy before the trip, but being there and seeing it in person saddened me because of their attitude toward female babies. We were told that if the firstborn baby was female, it was disposed of. That was mind-boggling, that they would knowingly and willingly kill those babies. They justified it with the belief that boys were more likely to support their aging parents later on in life. I'm not sure that theory holds water, but that's what we were told. For those of us working every day to save babies, this policy was hard to get our heads around. Having too many people is an issue we're facing as a species, but their "solution" was quite brutal. China eventually modified the policy to allow parents in rural areas to have two children if the first was a female. In 2021, for the first time since the 1980s, families in China could have up to three children. This is due partly to a steep decline in the birthrate. As of 2022, China still has more than 1.4 billion people. While the rate of population growth has declined, the overall population is still rising.

Two years after our trip to China, in 1987, we were invited on a second trip, this time to Hungary and Russia. Most of the original group members who traveled to China signed up for this one as well. Our first stop was Budapest where we visited with doctors and nurses at a modern NICU. We were impressed with the facilities, although they didn't have the technology we were used to back in the states. One thing that did stand out was the discrimination that the Hungarian people, including the medical staff, showed toward the local gypsies. There was a large population of gypsies in Hungary at the time and they were treated as second- or third-class citizens.

After our stay in Budapest, we flew to Moscow where our tour guide was a female neonatologist. We immediately got a taste of the harsh conditions in Russia. The hotel was quite modest and had no air conditioning, even though we were there during the intense heat of July. To get a little relief from the heat, we opened the windows, but then we were quickly attacked by some of the largest flies I'd ever seen. It was not the most pleasant way to start the trip, however, there were a lot of positives about the city.

First and foremost, the architecture of Moscow was amazingly impressive. The highlight of Moscow was attending the Bolshoi Ballet. We were touring Red Square and heard that the ballet was performing that night. Because our group was 40 people, we didn't think we'd be able to get enough tickets, but as soon as we asked around, we were surrounded by Muscovites who were able to supply us with plenty of tickets. Amazingly, we were at the most prestigious ballet in the world that night and seated across from Prime Minister Michael Gorvachev and his wife Raisa.

We were disappointed that we didn't visit any hospitals in Moscow. When we inquired about it, we were told that the hospitals were closed during summer for cleaning. We couldn't imagine how hospitals full of sick people could completely close down. We realized they didn't care about health care as much as they did their military and space program, which is where they focused their money. They also advised us not to exchange dollars for rubles but, being brash Americans, we did it anyway and had no problems. In fact, the day that we arrived, the waitress at the hotel arranged for us to make the exchange.

After Moscow, we flew to Kryiv and finally were able to visit a hospital that was run by a pediatric surgeon. Considering the limited resources and the outdated equipment he had, the doctor was doing a great job. We also visited a hospital close to the Chernobyl nuclear facility, the site of the worst nuclear disaster in history that occurred in 1986. Only

Chernobyl and the Fukushima nuclear accident in 2011 were rated at seven, the maximum severity on the International Nuclear Event Scale. It is estimated that more than 200,000 people died and many babies were born with congenital birth defects due to radiation exposure.

We all knew how bad Chernobyl had been, but they fed us a lot of government propaganda that downplayed the impact. Most of us laughed when we read the statement they provided to us. Our reaction to the document almost caused an international crisis. Our team leader had to apologize to the officials, who had become extremely upset with us.

From Kryiv, we traveled to St. Petersburg for the last leg of the trip. We were able to see another ballet performance during a white night—a night with no darkness because we were so far north. We also toured the Hermitage Museum and the Summer Palace, which were both impressive. Subsequently, the trip ended after traveling by train to Helsinki, Finland, where we had the opportunity to debrief from our experience.

Chapter 10
My Life in Sports

As I talked about earlier in the book, I spent my childhood in Colombia playing soccer. We called it futbol (as does every other nation in the world, except in the U.S. where American football is king). Even though football is as American as apple pie, during the time I've lived in the states, soccer has grown by leaps and bounds. I was lucky to find a good group of adults in Orlando who enjoyed the game as much as I did.

I played soccer in Orlando for almost two decades on a team we called the Blue Brothers. Ours was an international team with players mostly from Europe, North Africa, and South America. We did have a few Americans on the team as well. As far as winning, we were just an average team, but we felt accomplished to be playing a sport into our late 40s. I guess because I'd played defender as a kid, I continued playing in the sweeper position as an adult as well.

> As the members of the Blue Brothers got older and the teams we played against had players in their 20s, some of the games got pretty physical. Sure, it was just a game, but we still wanted to win.

Gregor, kneeling, 2nd from the right

On a few occasions, I ended up in the hospital with broken ribs. My radiology friends knew when I showed up for X-rays that I'd been playing soccer. I remember one episode when we were playing in the rain and as I jumped up to head the ball, my face collided against the head of an Italian player. He had a "testa dura," which means hard head in Italian. My left eyebrow opened up and blood was going everywhere. Fortunately, the field was behind a hospital (or maybe we planned it that way on purpose or subconsciously). As I stood there trying to stop the bleeding, I called a plastic surgeon friend of mine and asked him to meet me at the emergency room of the hospital next to our soccer field.

I told him I had a pretty severe eyebrow laceration, and he graciously agreed to come and stitch me up. When I arrived at the ER in a soccer uniform with a muddy face and blood pouring from my eyebrow, I saw a nurse that I knew. I just said, "Hi, it's Dr. Alexander. Dr. Price is going to meet me here to suture my wound."

She looked me up and down and replied. "I'm sorry but I know Dr. Alexander, and you sure don't look like him." After I cleaned up my face, I was able to convince her that it was me. Dr. Price arrived shortly after, did a great job on the stitches, and probably wondered when I was going to stop playing soccer.

Toward the end of my soccer "career," we were playing on another field in front of a different hospital. (I'm pretty sure we did arrange that one on purpose.) One of the players on the other team was a friend of mine and an adult urologist in his 40s. Even at that fairly young age, he'd had some serious heart issues and ended up having several stents placed in his coronary arteries. It was a successful operation and he continued to play. I think he loved the game so much because he was such a highly skilled player. He had been given the clearance to play soccer by his cardiologist, and he was super excited to be back on the pitch. Sure enough, in his first game back, he dribbled the ball almost effortlessly into the box and scored a beautiful goal with a shot into the side netting. I wasn't at all surprised since I'd seen him do that many times before.

> After the goal, he went down to the ground in a kind of exhausted celebration. After a few moments, he wasn't getting up, so we went to check on him. I was hoping he was just tired from his scoring run, but I quickly assessed he was in cardiorespiratory arrest. I immediately administered CPR and was able to get him breathing and his heart beating again while the captain of the team sprinted to the ER to get more medical support.

The medical team arrived quickly and transported him to the ER, where he had another arrest. This time, he didn't respond to CPR. They tried every other means and effort in the ER but nothing helped. Sadly, he passed away right there with his teammates watching helplessly.

Most likely, he had ruptured the heart muscle and nothing could have been done to save him. We were all in a bit of shock. As I reflected on the tragedy, the only positive aspect was that his very last act on this earth, before going to the other dimension, was scoring a goal in a game he adored.

A few weeks after the death of my friend, I was playing soccer again, this time on a different field. I collided in the air… again… against a player that was at least 50 pounds heavier than me. I knew instinctively as we flew through the air that it was not going to end well. On the way down to the ground, my right elbow was tucked below my chest and was the first body part to hit the ground. The impact fractured two ribs, and I was breathless for about 30 seconds while the rest of the players surrounded me but didn't know how to perform CPR. During those long 30 seconds, I thought to myself that I better begin to breathe on my own or I would be the next player to die. I also promised myself never to play soccer again, that is, if I lived.

Fortunately, I did begin to breathe again, and I stuck by my decision to stop playing soccer. I've always loved sports and staying physically fit, and that is when I made the decision to train for marathons. I'm not sure why I chose one of the most grueling sports, but I did. I think I was mostly inspired by all of those babies we'd cared for and their tenacity and fight for survival.

From Soccer to Marathons

BOSTON MARATHON

Before my first Boston Marathon, I had the opportunity to spend a weekend at a retreat with one of my idols, Tony Robbins. His positive energy and motivational speaking is inspirational. Part of the weekend was demonstrating the power of the mind over the body, and he got us to walk barefoot over hot coals for a few feet. Weekends like that are fuel for the soul, and I was invigorated to continue making a difference in my personal and professional life.

For training, I joined a group at the best running store in Orlando, the Track Shack. Owners Jon and Betsy Hughes had linked up with Jeff Galloway, who was a former U.S. Olympic marathoner. His program for those of us who were just starting was to run for 10 minutes then walk for one minute, then repeat that.

Our group got together in Winter Park, a suburb of Orlando, on weekends between 4 a.m. and 6 a.m., depending on the distance we were training for that day. We had people from all ages and backgrounds but everyone had one thing in common: a positive mental attitude (PMA). Because of my accent and previous soccer experience, most of the runners in our group thought I was a former Polish soccer player. I'm not sure how that rumor started, but eventually, they learned that I was a baby doctor. I ended up developing strong friendships and connections with my fellow runners as we became comfortable with each other and shared stories of our personal and professional lives. I think the camaraderie with my fellow runners propelled me to be able to quickly progress from two miles to a full marathon of 26.2 miles.

> My very first marathon was at Disney World, and I was able to complete the entire race. Afterward, I felt like I was on top of the world, but then I began to cry.

I'm sure there were many emotions welling up in me—maybe going all the way back to my childhood—that caused that type of reaction, but also knowing that only one percent of the world's population had completed a marathon was a key reason I was swelling with pride. All in all, I ran in 16 marathons over a period of 20 years. I did five in Florida, one each in New York, San Diego, Chicago, Washington, D.C., and two Boston Marathons, which is probably the most recognized run in the world. The rest of them were international: Quebec, Canada; Venice, Italy; Stockholm, Sweden; Prague; Czechoslovakia; and Rio de Janeiro, Brazil. The excitement of being in a foreign country was always inspirational, and running marathons was a good excuse to travel the world.

I was never a fast runner, but I always had the endurance needed for the completion. My speed averaged about 10 or 11 minutes per mile and my personal best time was 4 hours and 22 minutes in the Tampa Marathon. Like many runners, my favorite was the Boston Marathon because of the long, rich history and prestige. There's also an amazing amount of encouragement from the spectators, especially the ladies at

Wesley College with their screams and kisses.

> During a training run in 2010, I developed excruciating pain in my back and left leg. I had difficulty sitting, walking, sleeping, and working, and for weeks, my personal and professional life were a challenge.

My appetite disappeared, and I lost 25 pounds. Something was obviously very wrong with me and I was diagnosed with a herniated disc at L2 to L3. I took a lot of pain medications and had epidural injections, but the pain remained intolerable. Eventually, I had two surgeries. Two, because the first one didn't correct the problem. Twelve days after the first surgery, the fantastic neurosurgeon Dr. Nizam Razack performed the second procedure, and to this day, I believe he saved my life. He even delved into the details of my daily routine and encouraged me to trade in my stick shift Porsche for an automatic. He wanted me to alleviate the pressure at the spine when I was changing gears.

Dr. Razack also advised me not to run anymore. I followed his first advice and traded in my Porsche, but I still wanted to run one more marathon. A friend of mine, Jon Hughes, was able to get me a spot and number in the 2014 Boston Marathon. This was the year after the domestic terrorist attack by Dzhokhar Tsarnaev and Tamerlan Tsarnaev, who planted two homemade pressure cooker bombs near the finish line of the race. Tragically, their bombs killed three people and injured hundreds of others, including 17 people who lost limbs.

There were more police and other law enforcement than I've ever seen on the scene for the 2014 race. A lot of tension was in the air, but the people of Boston were determined to get their race back on track. I had trained hard knowing it would be my last race. My emotions were all over the place as I competed on that cold, rainy day. I was so thrilled to finish the race and the first photo of me wearing my finishing medal was sent to Dr. Razack with an apology and a statement that I promised never to run marathons again.

With both soccer and marathons being past history in my life, I began doing daily power walks of between 4–6 miles to stay in shape. I also

used a paddleboard to add a little variety to my exercise routine.

Olympic Honor

In 2001, I received an extraordinary surprise. One of the chaplains at the hospital had submitted my name to the U.S. Olympic Committee to be considered as an Olympic torch carrier. There were thousands of submissions, but somehow I was chosen to carry the torch. What an amazing honor!

My route was actually very close to my house in Winter Park, Florida. I was assigned to carry the Olympic torch for about a quarter of a mile. At first, I was disappointed by the short distance, but then appreciated it because it was quite heavy. As I ran, I was cheered on by a substantial group of local people. My section of the run was also televised. I was also told that for a small fee I could keep the torch. Each runner has his or her own torch, and it's really the flame itself that is the important part. As long as the fire is transferred from one torch to the next without going out, then the mission is successful. Of course, I paid the small fee and kept the torch. It is proudly displayed in my house to this day.

Chapter 11
The Big Day

After eight years of fundraising, planning, and construction, the new hospital was almost ready. It all happened with great fanfare on Arnold's 60th birthday, September 10, 1989. Our long-time dream had finally come to fruition, and it was a feeling I cannot express in words. When we moved in, we had 79 beds. Adjacent to our newborn unit and children's facility was a brand new tower that had the capacity for 5,000 deliveries per year.

The day before we officially moved the babies and children, we let the community tour the hospital. More than three thousand people attended that day, and we were all beaming with pride at what we had accomplished. But we also were keenly aware there was much more work to be done.

I remember vividly the morning we moved our babies to the new facility. We were excited and incredibly organized and were able to accomplish this task in four hours without any problems whatsoever. The new hospital was only two blocks away, but anytime you move patients, there's a great risk. We utilized ambulances and our team performed their own kind of miracles in the transition. I believe God was guiding us that day and smiling on our success.

As we settled in, my relationship with Mr. Palmer became stronger and more special. We met frequently to talk about the care being provided. He always looked forward to what challenges were ahead of us, and he asked my opinion about how we could improve our services and expand. Mr. Palmer did so much more than raise money and put his name on the building. He was very deeply involved and cared intently about what we were doing. That was so clear in many ways, one of which was when he brought friends and family members on the tours. Then, his wife Winnie became a board member of the hospital system. They cared so much about the success of our facility and realized that the health care members (doctors, nurses, etc.) needed to have their concerns and needs addressed in order to deliver excellence of care.

> Because of my relationship with the Palmers and for being one of founding members, I became the ambassador of the medical staff. I was honored to be the point person between the Palmers and the hospital. The relationship was professional, but we also became very close friends.

At first, we thought that we had built a facility big enough to handle our current load and future growth, however, we definitely miscalculated. We had created a Field of Dreams for parents and babies. We built it and they came, in droves. More and more babies were being delivered and treated at the new state-of-the-art hospital. After a few years, we realized it was not enough to meet the growing needs of our area. We needed yet another new hospital to handle our exponential growth.

Dr. Alexander with Winnie and Arnold Palmer

Winnie Palmer Hospital for Women and Babies

The success of the Arnold Palmer Hospital for Children and Babies was so gratifying and amazing. However, it became so popular that everyone in the region wanted to have their babies delivered there.

Mrs. Palmer was always in touch with the pulse of the hospital operations. She was deeply concerned that the needs of the staff were met and fulfilled. She called me often to ask how we could make our facility better from the perspective of the medical staff. I welcomed her involvement because it came from her heart. This was one of her passions and a testament to her commitment to helping others.

Sadly, she became ill with cancer. Even during those difficult times, she was sending Fortune 500 executives and others potential benefactors to us for tours in hopes that they would donate. I was lucky to have the opportunity to stay connected with this wonderful, warm, and caring lady even as she was battling cancer and until her death on November 20, 1999, from ovarian cancer. When we finally began the project of a women and babies hospital a few years after her death, I knew in my heart that it should be named in her honor.

I eventually was named chairman of the Arnold Palmer Foundation and subsequently the chairman of the Orlando Health Foundation. The CEO of the entire hospital system at the time was a former nurse of mine who started her career with me in the 1970s. Another nurse I had previously worked with became the president of both hospitals. It was great to see former staff members climb the administrative ladder to become top executives. I believe the lessons they learned at our baby unit helped to inspire them to reach these positions.

> Winnie Palmer Hospital for Women and Babies opened in 2006 with a capacity to deliver more than 10,000 babies per year with beds for 112 intensive care babies.

The initial build-out was nine floors with the 10th and 11th floors left unfinished as shell space for future expansion. Only a few years later, because of increased deliveries and the need for more beds, we expanded the neonatal unit to the 11th floor. It cost $13 million, but it gave us an additional 30 beds for a total capacity of 142 beds. It still amazes me that we only had 24 beds in the NICU when Arnold Palmer took that first tour. We had grown so large in a relatively short time and had become the largest neonatal care unit under one roof in the world.

With the new hospital up and running with state-of-the-art facilities for babies, the name of the original hospital was changed and shortened to the Arnold Palmer Children's Hospital. It was utilized for children with different types of medical conditions, and because we didn't want to duplicate services at both hospitals, we built a super-modern NICU at Winnie Palmer and connected the hospitals with a bridge. I always envisioned that bridge as an umbilical cord between the two facilities.

The Development of the ECMO Program

It was the mid-80s when we were admitting a number of term and post-term newborn infants who were afflicted with pulmonary hypertension. Basically, their blood was being shunted away from the lungs through two pathways inside and outside the heart before it could reach their lungs to mix with oxygen. The circulation pattern these babies experience is the same that occurs during their fetal life. Babies who experience this condition are among the sickest that we specialists try to save. A significant number of them kept failing the most aggressive medical support including breathing machines, medications to support their blood pressure, and inhaled gas to relax the pulmonary vessels to allow more blood to reach their lungs.

I was aware of a technological support that scientists had been working on for decades that might provide a solution. It was an artificial membrane that allowed for oxygen delivery to the circulating blood as well as carbon dioxide exchange. The technology was called ECMO (extracorporeal membrane oxygenation), and it had been used successfully in California in the mid-70s by a pediatric surgeon named Dr. Robert Bartlett on a baby who aspirated her bowel movements (meconium) into her lungs. Her name was Esperanza, which means "hope" in Spanish. The ECMO was the key to her survival.

> Based on this positive outcome on Esperanza, other centers were established to offer this technology and were having significant success in the babies they treated. The state of Florida at the academic and private level were very skeptical of ECMO and didn't want to invest money, resources, and personnel in this endeavor. We were tired of and very concerned about transferring these critical babies to other states with the risk of them getting sicker or not surviving the move from one hospital to another across state lines.

With the support of my partners, the staff, and hospital administration, I decided to develop the first ECMO program dedicated exclusively to newborn infants in Florida. A grant for a half-million dollars from the Variety Club Foundation allowed us to get the necessary equipment. We flew to the University of Michigan, where Dr. Bartlett had relocated, to get the comprehensive medical and technological training. Before we could use the procedure on human babies, we had to practice on lambs. We had to perform the ECMO successfully on 10 lambs before we could take that next step to babies. Because we did not have any animals on our campus nor the facilities to do procedures on animals, we used a room in the adult morgue. We carried lamb after lamb to a room full of cadavers and placed them in our designated room. If the morgue was crowded, we were able to use a room provided by a local veterinarian during the weekends when his office was closed.

Once we were comfortable that our success rate was as close to perfection as possible, we waited for our first real patient. Ironically, our first patient had the same medical condition as Esperanza. She was transferred from Tampa to our hospital in August of 1989. Our first procedure was successful and she survived and thrived.

At the time of my departure from the Arnold and Winnie Palmer hospitals, we had treated close to 450 babies using ECMO with an overall survival of between 85-90%. Based on our pioneering success through the years, more programs were established. We were so proud of being the leader in establishing the first artificial heart and lung program in Florida.

Transportation Advances

During the next couple of decades, after the Arnold Palmer Hospital for Children and Babies opened and was thriving, we developed an extraordinary land transport system using state-of-the-art ambulances built specifically for babies. We also created strong air transportation capabilities by utilizing helicopters and airplanes when travel by road was not possible. Our transport team of nurses and respiratory therapists kept the system clicking like a well-oiled machine, which was not an easy task. It required custom-made stretchers integrated with transport incubators, respirators, and additional equipment so we could move critically ill newborns quickly and safely.

> One factor we had to consider was excessive noise and vibration, as we believed these factors were detrimental to the health of our babies. Our team members were pioneers in protecting these infants from harmful sounds, too much shaking and movement, or any outside forces that might cause potential brain injury. We took every precaution we could to ensure that transporting infants by land or air was as safe as possible for these fragile lives.

In 1995, we hired a former pediatric resident, Dr. Jose Perez, who trained under our supervision and underwent neonatal training at Emory in Atlanta. Dr. Perez brought in fresh ideas about the care of our infants from "that's the way we do it with great results" to evidence-based medicine.

Initially, I was skeptical of his concepts but decided to embrace Dr. Perez's philosophies, and soon, we were witnessing greater outcomes in both survival and quality of life for our babies. One of the most significant changes was putting more emphasis on the role of the parents, siblings, and family members. We began letting families visit 24 hours a day and participate in the healing of the souls of our babies through touching, massage, and Kangaroo Care, which was developed in my home country of Colombia by doctors who didn't have enough facilities to care for preterm infants. It's called Kangaroo Care because of how the mother kangaroo keeps her babies (Joey's) in her pouch.

> When a baby was stable enough, at even just one pound, we would take them out of the incubator and put them on their mother's chest. We learned that tender loving care is vital in the healing process and we started incorporating every form of TLC we could think of.

Parents were able to talk to their babies, read stories, and we even invited harpists and guitarists to play music for our babies, parents, and staff. We noticed that with the parent's presence, the oxygen levels and vital signs of our babies improved. That connection and interaction with the baby's families created strong ties that remained after discharge from the neonatal unit and for the rest of our patient's lives. If the parents were out of town, they could designate a nurse or volunteer to show these babies loving attention. Love can work as well as medicine. As I always say, it's not how much you know but how much you care.

Meeting Tiger Woods

Through my personal relationship with the Palmers and being a foundation member of the hospital, I was able to present an award to the winner of the Arnold Palmer Invitational golf tournament. I gave the award on behalf of the babies and children from the hospital.

Standing on the 18th green next to Mr. Palmer and surrounded by the press and a host of VIPs was a surreal experience for me. I was flooded with emotions of coming from South America with nothing but a Colombian medical degree and having the opportunity to stand with the king of golf to present an award on national television. I thought about my difficult childhood and how hard I had worked to overcome so many obstacles. That work paid off for me, for the babies I loved, and for the Palmers, who were so instrumental in making our vision a reality.

Of course, Mr. Palmer's days of competitive golf were behind him, but each year I had the opportunity to present the hospital award to many world famous golfers. On eight occasions, Tiger Woods won the Arnold Palmer Invitational, and I gave the award to him most of those times. Being in the presence of Arnold Palmer and Tiger Woods—the legend and golf's new royalty—was such an honor, and soon I became close to Woods and his wife, Elin.

My friendship with Mr. Palmer continued to develop and grow throughout the years. I visited him in Latrobe, Pennsylvania, where he was born and grew up. His father was the groundskeeper at the country club in Latrobe, a course that Mr. Palmer subsequently purchased. His daughter, Amy Saunders, gave me a tour of all the memorabilia inside a huge hangar next to the Latrobe Country Club, where all seven of his golf major trophies were kept. When Mr. Palmer was awarded the Gold Congressional Medal of Honor on September 11, 2012, I was among a handful of hospital members invited to the ceremony at the Capitol Building in Washington D.C. He was the sixth athlete to receive such an honor.

Our friendship lasted more than 30 years. I had the privilege to visit Mr. Palmer one last time, just 12 days before his death. He was very frail but, appropriately, sitting in a golf cart with that familiar sparkle in his eyes. We embraced and he asked me about the hospital.

> "Gregor," he said, in his typical sincere way. "I want you to promise me that you will always continue to work to grow the excellence of medical care at the hospital." I looked at this man who had opened the door to so many miracles and said, "Yes sir. I am happy to keep that promise."

He smiled and knew that I was a man of my word. And I kept that promise until my last day at the Winnie Palmer Hospital for Women and Babies on August 26, 2019, at 4:00 pm.

Arnold Palmer died on September 25, 2016, at the age of 87, but his legacy in healthcare will remain through the lives of thousands of babies, children, and high-risk mothers. To the world he is the King of Golf, but to all of us at the hospitals and to humanity, he is the King of Hearts.

More Golf

My relationship with golf and famous golfers grew out of my friendship with the Palmers. I met many of the world's best golfers and developed a special relationship with Tiger Woods and Annika Sorenstam.

At the end of one of the Arnold Palmer Invitational tournaments, I finally got to meet the legend himself. After a short, congratulatory speech on behalf of the hospital and presenting him with the award, I also gave Tiger a special drawing from one of our little patients. He

Tiger Woods, Dr. Alexander and Arnold Palmer

accepted gracefully with a smile and handshake.

A little later, as I was standing next to Mr. Palmer, he waved Tiger over, away from the media, for a photo with the three of us. Mr. Palmer looked at him and said, "Tiger, please get a picture next to Dr. Alexander. You may need him in the future."

> Those words turned out to be prophetic and became a reality a few years later when Tiger and his wife Elin visited our facility, the Winnie Palmer Hospital for Women and Babies. After a short tour, they were assured that Elin and her baby would receive the best medical care in a private and safe environment.

Once the decision was made by Elin and Tiger to have the baby at our facility, we planned for an early morning delivery by cesarean section due to obstetric (OB) medical and fetal indications. I worked with the hospital administration and selected the neonatal team, nurse, and respiratory therapist to assist me during the delivery and subsequent care. We converted one of the rooms adjacent to the OB area into a small neonatal unit with a radiant warmer, respirator, and all the necessary equipment to provide the highest intensive care, if needed.

Dr. Alexander and Tiger Woods

At the time, Tiger was the top golfer in the world, and we had to have extremely tight security and provide him with privacy from the press. Once Tiger finished playing the 2007 U.S. Open, he flew overnight and shortly after his arrival, Sam Alexis Woods was born. Despite her early gestation and low birth weight, Sam was born with healthy lungs, and after a short period of nasal cannula oxygen, support she was breathing normally. A few days later, after mild transient jaundice and full feedings with adequate temperature regulation, she went home with her parents.

Through our interactions at golf tournaments and during Elin's pregnancy, I had developed a good relationship with Tiger and was fortunate to have the opportunity to talk with him one-on-one at the hospital. I was impressed that he acted like a normal person despite his fame and fortune. Like most new fathers, he called his mother and his in-laws in Sweden shortly after Sam's delivery. He also insisted on staying in the room with Elin, despite us offering a quiet room with full amenities next door to her.

During one of our conversations, he found out I was a marathon runner, and we discussed running and training techniques. It was such a special time for him and his family, but also for me as I got to know more about this incredible athlete and new father.

My relationship with the Woods continued as their son Charlie was born a few years later in our facility with my attendance and medical care. He was born without complications.

I saw Tiger off and on and, of course, at the Arnold Palmer Invitationals. On one of those occasions, we embraced in the middle of the award ceremony and he asked me how my running was progressing. I was a little bit shocked that he remembered but realized that he's human just like the rest of us and takes a genuine interest in others.

He and I have stayed in touch through the years, even after his divorce to Elin. He is always warm and friendly, and on behalf of his children, we received a generous donation to the hospital. One of the rooms in our neonatal unit is named in honor of the Woods family. To this day, I stay connected with Elin who had visited the hospital with Sam and Charlie and still keeps me posted about their lives.

My connection with Annika Sorenstam began when she chose the Winnie Palmer Hospital for Women and Babies in 2009 to deliver her first baby Ava, and she requested my attendance to the delivery. Annika had a normal, natural birth at term gestation and without complications, and Ava was born healthy and happy. However, the situation was different with her second child. A few years after Ava was born, I received a concerned phone call from Annika. During her second pregnancy and at 27 weeks gestation, she had vaginal bleeding due to premature separation of the placenta. She had an emergency cesarean section and her son Will was born with immaturity of his lungs. This required respiratory support and administration of a surfactant to mature his lungs. His stabilization was done by a very skillful partner of mine, Dr. Michael McMahan, along with the neo team. Two days later, I had the opportunity to meet Will and co-manage his care for a few weeks.

My relationship with Annika and her husband Mike McGee solidified during Will's hospital stay until he was discharged. Since then, Annika has been a great supporter of the hospital. The last time I saw her was at Mr. Palmer's funeral in Latrobe. Both of her children are healthy, and despite Will being born premature with immature lungs, his health is perfect.

Dr Alexander

There Are Not Enough Hours,
Words, or Paper To Convey My
Emotions or More Importantly
What You Have Achieved In The
Founding of NeoIntensive Care,
It's Vision, Accomplishments And
Impact On Tens of Thousands of Lives:
Babies, Parents, Family : Staff.

Forever Loved
— Christine Naylor RN
LEVEL III NIGHTS

Chapter 12

Miracle Babies

In my medical career, I witnessed many miracles in the tiniest of babies that showed a tremendous will to survive. I also saw close to term and full-term infants survive even though they arrived at our neonatal unit in moribund stage. They lived and thrived because of the technological advances developed in the last few decades and definitely because of our willingness to provide them the best care, not only from the medical point of view but from our passionate and compassionate care.

Each of us cared for the babies as if they were part of us. As I stated before, we became "emotional billionaires" by being able to care for so many babies for more than four decades. Their souls will remain in our hearts and minds forever. Through them, we made the world a better place.

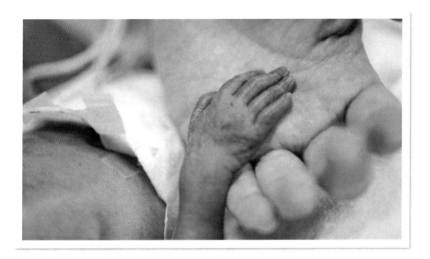

A Miracle Baby

It was the mid-80s when I was called to attend the delivery of a baby by emergency cesarean section. The premature baby was six weeks early at 34 weeks gestation and in distress. The initial delivery went well but then turned for the worst. Once he was born, we noticed he was blue with no heartbeat or breathing effort. Essentially, in medical terms, the baby was in cardiorespiratory arrest.

I proceeded to perform a full cardiopulmonary rescue. We breathed for the baby using a face mask but got no response. Without difficulty, I was able to place a tube down the baby's trachea and administer breaths with oxygen as the team nurse provided cardiac compressions.

Because of the lack of heartbeat and respirations, I placed a catheter inside of the umbilical cord vein and over a period of a few minutes, gave intravenous epinephrine to stimulate his heart activity. After 15 minutes with no signs of life, we sadly stopped our attempts to revive him and I pronounced the baby dead.

We removed the endotracheal tube and umbilical catheter and wrapped this beautiful baby boy in blankets. With the approval of the parents, I baptized the baby and handed him to the parents to hold and kiss. Pictures were taken and many tears were shed. After explaining to the parents about our efforts and expressing my sorrow to them, I left to go to the neonatal unit to continue the daily care of my patients.

More than an hour later, my beeper rang asking me to come to see this baby boy. I was surprised and a bit dismayed but I went. Just a minute before they called me, the baby had turned pink and had established a normal heart rate and was breathing. He was also crying. I couldn't believe what I was witnessing! Inside a transport incubator, we transferred this apparently healthy, 4-lb., 3-oz. baby to our NICU.

We were able to feed him maternal breast milk a few hours later and place him in a crib. His physical and neurological exam was normal as well as his brain ultrasound and CT scan. When we decided it was safe to release him from our care, the baby was discharged to his parents with the typical pediatrician and newborn clinic follow-up scheduled.

> I kept in touch with his family for the first two years of his life, and I was informed that he was developing like any normal baby. Yet, we all knew how special the miracle baby was and how resilient tiny humans can be. He somehow came back from the dead, and I often reflect on how fortunate I was to witness this miracle.

By all medical accounts, the recovery of this baby cannot be explained using any kind of logic. First of all, he had died after all of our efforts and using every procedure at our disposal. His death was witnessed by the nurses helping me. Then, for an hour, he had no heartbeat or breathing, as far as we knew. Perhaps the epinephrine we had administered had some delayed effect. Yet, any medical professional will tell you that there should have been brain damage. Yet, there was none.

This event, as well as many others, deepened my faith that God is always watching and playing a role in our daily lives, even when we don't realize it. Maybe especially when we're not aware of it. Could the connection with the parents as they held their child had something to do with his rebirth? It's as good of an answer as I can come up with. Again, I cannot explain it, but I know that it happened and I know that I witnessed a miracle that day.

Dr. A

I am truly sad to know that I won't have the pleasure of working with you anymore. Your passion, drive and love for these babies is really what motivated me to work even harder making sure the babies get the best care. You are truly an inspiration to all and will truly be missed. You have left your legacy at Winnie and it is a great one.
Best wishes in your future endeavors.
— Cortni

P.S. Thank you again for my grinch christmas tree ornament. I love it!

One More Miracle

I vividly remember the first and only international transportation of one of our babies. This event occurred in the early 2000s when I got a call from the president of the Arnold and Winnie Palmer hospitals. She was notified by the president and CEO of SeaWorld Orlando that a husband and wife, who were trainers of the famous orca Shamu, had delivered a premature baby in Panama City, Central America. They wanted us to transport her to our facility. The baby's name was Trinity.

The couple was at the beach in Panama when the wife went into premature labor and had vaginal bleeding at 28 to 30 weeks gestation. She was flown by helicopter to the capital, Panama City, where she delivered a two-pound infant by cesarean section. Trinity was connected to a respirator in the neonatal unit at the hospital and was struggling for her life.

I totally agreed with the request from the parents and began assembling a team—a NICU nurse and respiratory therapist—to assist me in the process. We contacted an air ambulance company to support the logistics of the transport. We were ready to go, but to our surprise, the SeaWorld Health Insurance Company was denying coverage claiming they couldn't understand the need to transport this baby to the United States. They were trying to equate neonatal intensive care in the U.S. to Panama. While they do have good care in Panama, it really does not compare to the expertise and facilities we have in this country.

Apparently, the CEO of SeaWorld Orlando had to call the CEO of the health insurance company with threats to cease coverage for the entire SeaWorld company to finally get an approval. When Trinity was just a few days old, we flew over 1,300 miles to retrieve her. The parents were so excited and relieved when they saw us.

At the airport in Panama, with Trinity inside the plane receiving intensive care, we ran into problems. One of the immigration officers came aboard and told us we couldn't leave the country because we were missing a document. Calmly, and in Spanish, I told this man that if he prevented us from leaving, Trinity would not survive and he was going to cause an international problem between the United States and Panama. He thought about it for a few seconds and then accepted my threat and we flew away with a very stable but critical baby.

We brought Trinity to Orlando and admitted her into our facility where she survived but required two surgeries in our facility. One surgery was needed to close a tiny vessel outside her heart and the other to seal a spontaneous perforation of her small bowel.

The last time I saw Trinity and her mother was just a few years ago, and she was doing exceptionally well. I am so proud of my team and the support the hospital offered to make this outcome possible.

Chapter 13
Experience with the Spirit World

People speak of extra sensory perception (ESP), and as a doctor, I have always tried to use science to make sense of the world. However, I do believe in miracles, and I've also had some encounters where the only explanation seems to be intervention from a dimension we don't fully understand.

After my first year in Orlando, when the South African doctor was asked to leave and I was on my own, I worked 24/7 to keep up. I loved the hectic pace, but sometimes I would neglect my personal life. I was taking a day off at home and catching up with personal things like trimming my beard and mustache, which had gotten quite shaggy. In the process, I cut my nose. It started bleeding badly, so I called a friend who was a plastic surgeon and had an office only two blocks from the hospital. He was able to control the bleeding easily and laughed at me for overreacting. He just put a standard bandaid on it and sent me home. As I was driving by the hospital, I had a strange sensation that something was wrong. I couldn't shake the feeling, so I turned around and drove to the hospital. When I walked into the NICU, everyone was staring at a baby that was in cardiac arrest at that very moment. No one knew what to do and there was a lot of panic. They were so busy trying to revive the baby that they didn't see the underlying cause.

I quickly examined the baby and realized it had a collapsed lung. I placed a chest tube in the left lung and I was able to drain out the air. Almost immediately, the baby's heartbeat went back up and it started breathing more normally. Thankfully, the baby survived and went home a few weeks later. I often think about what would have happened if I

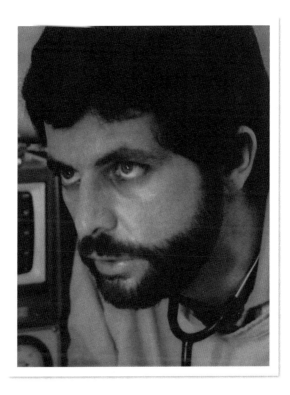

hadn't cut on my nose or if I had just driven straight home from the plastic surgeon. Some kind of outside force was alerting me that I was needed at the hospital. I can't explain it, but I know it happened.

I had another similar type of feeling during some time off when one of my partners was covering for me. There was a fire at the hospital, and they were about to evacuate the NICU. I was at home, but had an inner voice telling me that I was needed at the hospital. I called to check on things, and they told me about the fire and wondered how I knew. Of course, I jumped in the car and drove to the hospital to help, but they had contained it by the time I got there. Again, it was a feeling that just came to me out of the blue and I think it has something to do with the special bond I had created with the people and the NICU. Some things just can't be explained with logic.

The Traffic Ticket

One fairly typical day, I was in a meeting a few miles away from the hospital and got a call that I needed to assist in the delivery of a high-risk baby. I took the expressway because it was the fastest way. Soon, I was driving 80–100 miles per hour. I had a Porsche at the time, so it didn't seem like I was going that fast. Not to me anyway but definitely to the highway patrol. A policeman stopped me, but before he could ask me why I was driving so fast, I told him that I had been called into the hospital. I guess I wasn't convincing enough because he became quite skeptical and asked for the telephone number of the NICU. The receptionist wasn't aware that I'd been called. She told the cop that she didn't know anything, which didn't help my situation. Somehow I was able to convince the policeman to give me an escort to the hospital, but he still gave me the ticket, which I thought was extremely unfair. When I went to court and explained the situation to the judge, I hoped he would understand and let me off, but he still made me pay the fine. He then suggested that for the future I buy an official flashing red light for my car because it was legal for a doctor. I took his sage advice and had the lights installed on my Porsche. From then on, whenever I was called for an emergency, I could speed down the interstate with the lights flashing and without being stopped. I even changed my license plate to "Baby DR," so when the police saw me with those red lights and the license plate, they would leave me alone. I'll admit, there were a few times when I was tempted to turn on the red lights "just because," but I was always very honest and never used it except in emergencies. At least I had those few opportunities to drive that Porsche like a German on the Autobahn without speed limits.

Dr. Alexander, I chose Winnie as my number one spot after graduating because of the amazing work you have done here. I remember meeting you on my clinical rotation and immediately saw that you are not only a fantastic physician, but that you are also such a genuine person. Winnie is not the same without you and you are missed tremendously. I can honestly say that it has been both a privilege and honor to work beside you for the past year. I wish you and your family nothing but the best in the future and hope our paths may cross again one day.

Best regards,
Ashley

Chapter 14
Foundation Involvement

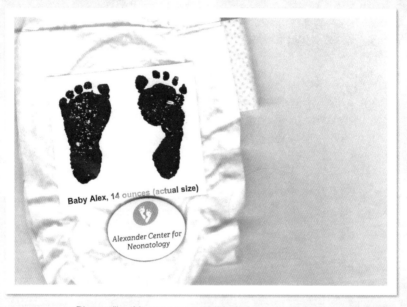

Baby Alex, 14 ounces (actual size)

Alexander Center for Neonatology

Diapers like this one were presented to groups touring the neonatal ICU

My involvement in foundation work began as soon as I arrived in Orlando and we had only six beds for our babies. This was during the late 1970s and the neonatal unit was growing in size and acuity. I quickly realized the extreme need to procure modern equipment to care for the growing number of babies. Funds were also needed to establish new programs and expand our physical facilities. The bottom line was our bottom line, meaning we had to raise our own money to fund these expansions. My philosophy has always been to lead by example, so I made a personal commitment to raise half of the total amount we needed.

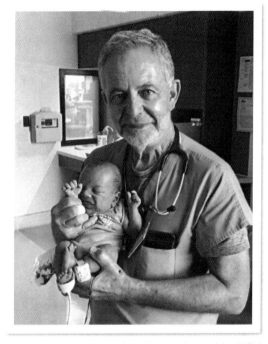

Dr. Alexander with a graduate of the NICU

Depending on what equipment we needed to purchase or what project we were working on determined how much we needed to raise. The first fundraiser we organized was for a vital piece of equipment—a state-of-the-art neonatal ambulance. Until then, we were utilizing commercial ambulance companies, which were generally not equipped to provide ideal transportation for babies. Also, they weren't always available on a moment's notice. That was a problem we needed to solve. We found a suitable neonatal ambulance for about $50,000, which was a bargain at the time.

I did some research and discovered that the March of Dimes had a grant program, and we met all of the criteria. I applied and was elated to be awarded the grant that covered about 75 percent of the cost. We were well on the way to adding a specialized ambulance to our facility.

As we got to know the amazing people who worked for the March of Dimes, some of us in the neonatal unit decided to show our support for them and thank them for their grant by participating in their annual fundraising walks of 20 kilometers (12.4 miles). We were among the few adults who made such a commitment.

Subsequently, I stayed involved with the March of Dimes and their ongoing efforts to decrease neonatal mortality. It was gratifying that the organization was focused on prevention of prematurity and the treatment of immature newborn lung disease by replacing a surfactant in the lungs of these preemies. This focus on treatment of premature babies was right in our wheelhouse so working with them was a great pleasure and beneficial to both organizations. Years later, in 1998, I received the distinction of being the March of Dimes "Citizen of the Year" and chairman of their walk event a few years later.

After we had moved into the Arnold Palmer Hospital for Children and Babies, a very successful way we generated financial support for the neonatal unit was from grateful relatives of babies we saved and cared for. A great example was Larry Phillips, who owned Phillip Buick in Leesburg, Florida. After we treated his grandson, Wade, Larry became one of the largest philanthropic donors of the hospital. In addition to his generous donations, he would come to the cafeteria every Christmas and pay for breakfast, lunch, and dinner for everyone that day. That kind of generosity strengthens one's faith in mankind and, for me, fueled my drive to make our hospitals the best in the world.

> Because of the financial success of our foundation, we were also able to set up a separate foundation to support the medical needs of at-risk mothers, babies, and children. We called it the Arnold Palmer Medical Center Foundation and I was the chairman for seven years from 2009-2017.

Dear Dr. Alexander,

I'm not sure what to say, except thank you. Thank you for being the first doctor to welcome me to the unit on my first day as a grad nurse, and for showing me that not all doctors were as intimidating as they seemed in nursing school. Thank you for always asking for my input during rounds and genuinely listening to what I had to say. You created a culture where we are able to advocate for our patients and actually be heard. You inspired me to be a more confident and assertive nurse. You encouraged me to ask questions and to always be eager to learn. You pushed us all to be better. Thank you for treating your nurses and RT's as colleagues and not subordinates, and for caring for us all as a NICU family. And thank you for caring for every single one of your patients as if they were your own child. I've never met anyone who loves their job as much as you. You truly found your calling, and there are so many

children alive today because of that. We should all aspire to be as passionate about something as you are about your tiny patients. As I continue my career as a nurse and a nurse practitioner, I will try to bring that level of passion to my own practice. I know I am a better nurse for having worked with you, and I will forever owe you a debt of gratitude for that. Please know that we will try our best to carry on your legacy, but you will always be our captain ♡

— Kelli

In spite of spending the bulk of my conscious life working 50 or more hours per week in the NICU, I remained very excited to spend additional hours participating and speaking at fundraising events for the hospitals. Very early on, I realized the power of giving tours of our facilities by bringing visitors and donors up close and personal to the babies in our care. I remember seeing how amazed and somewhat shocked visitors were when they saw those tiny babies. Some weighed less than one pound, between 12–14 ounces, and were born at just 22 to 24 weeks.

> People were always impressed by the resilience and tenacity these babies had to survive. I was able to show our potential donors that survival and quality of life was not only dependent on our advanced medical knowledge, techniques, and equipment but was also based on "healing of the soul" that was provided by our caregivers and the parents.

A great highlight of the tours was when I introduced visitors to nurses on our staff who had been our patients at one time. I had personally participated in their care as preemies, and when they grew up and became nurses, some of them returned to work with us and carry on our care of babies. At least seven or eight of those preemie babies came back to work in our NICU. One was from a set of triplets, and she was inspired by the care she had received. Whenever I gave the tour, I would introduce people to her because it was a touching, real-life human story.

Another inspirational young woman who came back to our NICU was delivered in the early 1990s. She was a full-term baby but her shoulders couldn't fit through the birth canal. With only her head sticking out, I placed a tube in her throat/trachea. This is something that, to my knowledge, had never been done. Her heartbeat went up and allowed us to use a different anesthesia. Placement of a tracheal tube under these circumstances is extremely difficult, but I believe God was guiding my hands because I was successful in the first attempt. Once the tube was in place, we began breathing for the baby by administering oxygen.

To my surprise, her face became pink and her heart rate normalized. Subsequently, the mother's pelvis relaxed and the baby delivered successfully. That became known informally as the new Alexander Method.

Two decades later, after going to nursing school, she came back to work with us and the staff to care for critical babies. As visitors came to tour our newborn unit, I would sometimes have her next to me telling them her remarkable story and echoing what Albert Einstein stated that "everything in life is a miracle."

A lot of the people who toured our facilities were successful local businessmen and women, but I also gave tours to a tremendous number of high profile individuals and celebrities such as President George H. Bush and First Lady Barbara Bush. When I was president of the hospital foundation, I also met actors Paul Newman, Michael J. Fox, and Charlton Heston; and singers Celine Dion, B.J. Thomas, Marie Osmond, Amy Grant, Pettula Clark, Justin Timberlake, and Darius Rucker of Hootie and the Blowfish. We hosted governors, senators, professional golfers, and CEOs of Fortune 500 companies. Most of them left the neonatal unit inspired by our commitment to our babies.

Dr. Alexander with President George H. Bush

Before he was into politics, Donald Trump came to visit the hospital in 2014. I gave him a tour of the facility and took him to the NICU. Like just about everyone else, he was impressed by the modern facilities and the quality of the care we rendered. He mentioned to Mr. Palmer that his daughter, Ivanka, had recently delivered a baby in a facility that was not as clean and modern as our hospital. He also paid me a huge compliment asking Mr. Palmer "where had he hired a doctor like me?" Mr. Palmer just smiled. Mr. Trump ended up leaving us a very generous donation for the hospital foundation.

NASCAR Meets Colombia

One of my favorites tours ever was for Betty Jean France, the wife of NASCAR founder Bill France, Sr. Being from Colombia, I had no idea how big the auto racing world was, but I was about to learn. After I gave the tour in 1999, Betty Jean France asked me to participate in an event at Halifax Hospital in Daytona, Florida. They were opening the pediatric floor, and most of the funding had come from NASCAR. Initially, I was reluctant to attend because I had been on call for 24 hours in our neonatal unit, but the president of the Arnold Palmer Foundation called and told me how important it was. He was quite adamant about it and suggested that I sleep in the backseat of his car during the ride to Daytona. As always, I accepted on behalf of helping the hospital.

When I arrived, I was greeted by Mrs. France and Mark Martin, who was one of the top NASCAR drivers at the time. There's still a photo of the three of us on the pediatric floor in that hospital. I was beginning to see how dedicated the Frances were to helping babies, so the relationship was growing fast, both on a professional and personal level.

Mrs. France knew I had never attended an auto race, so she invited me to be a guest of her and her husband at the Daytona 500 in the year 2000. I was honored by the invitation and intrigued to see what all the excitement was about, watching cars go round and round really fast. On the day of the race, I left Orlando at 9:00 am, thinking I'd have plenty of time to get to Daytona for the late morning start of the race. I should have known better because by 10:00 a.m. I was stuck in traffic. Mrs. France had given me her assistant's cell phone number, and I called to let them know I was going to be late. Apparently, for them, that was not an option. He asked where I was and told me to wait there. In what seemed like about five minutes, a state patrolman on motorcycle showed up with his sirens screaming and lights flashing. He said, "Doctor, follow me. We're going to proceed a few miles against traffic, then when we get to Daytona, we're going onto the race track and finally to your parking spot." I'd had police escorts before, but those were all for medical emergencies. I didn't know how much sway the Frances had with law enforcement.

Mark Martin, Mrs. Franz and Dr. Alexander

We cruised down the road without obstruction and arrived at Daytona in record time. As the patrolman promised, we pulled into the stadium. I've always wondered what those 200,000 NASCAR fans were thinking when they saw a motorcycle escorting a Porsche with a "Baby DR" license plate going around the track. It was definitely a surreal experience for me.

After I parked, I was led to the VIP skybox and greeted by Mrs. France. She introduced me to her husband and their family as well as the president of NBC and many other VIP guests. I didn't know how lucky I was at the time, but when I told my friends about it, they were all jealous of my experience. The France family continued to be major supporters of NICUs in Florida, and I will forever be grateful to them for their generosity. I remained friends with Mrs. France for many years and was saddened by her death in 2016.

More Foundation Work

As part of my foundation efforts and during my years as a marathon runner, I established a race to benefit our NICU. We named the race the "Miracle Miles"' in honor of our babies. The race was initially funded by Chick-fil-A and subsequently sponsored by Panera Bread. The course was a 15K (9.3 miles) that began at the Arnold Palmer Children's Hospital campus and meandered through the streets of downtown Orlando. Our competing hospitals such as Florida Hospital/Advent Health held numerous runs, but Miracle Miles was the only race in our entire medical system. The greatest aspect of the race was bringing the focus of prematurity and high-risk newborn care to Central Florida and showcasing the incredible advances of increased survival year over year as well as improvement in quality of life for these babies.

> Each year, we grew in participation and the race began to draw thousands of runners for our cause. Since it was also the only 15K (9.3 miles) in the region, it attracted some serious runners who were training for full marathons and ultramarathons. During the 16 years we ran the Miracle Miles race, we raised close to a million dollars, which, as always, we used for more equipment purchases.

Ironically, the very first race and most of the subsequent ones were won in the female category by Michelle Kendall-Krueger, who was a former premature twin we had cared for in the 1970s. When she signed up, she had no idea that I was the founder and organizer of this event. At the awards ceremony, her mother made us both aware of the connection and the story ended up being published in *Runner's World* magazine under the title, "The Human Race." Michelle kept winning each year except the years when she was pregnant.

Dr. Alexander with Michelle Kendall-Krueger

After so many successful years, the foundation decided to transition to a two-mile walk at SeaWorld in Orlando and change the name to the "Walk for Winnie" in honor of Arnold Palmer's widow. Most of the walkers were former graduates of the neonatal unit and their families.

Under my involvement and leadership, we also organized reunions with our former patients and families every five years at one of the major state parks and sometimes at SeaWorld. Some of those reunions drew more than a thousand patients and family members. Those days were the highlight of my career as I witnessed the miracle of life for more than 90 percent of our patients. Also the vast majority of those tiny babies that we saved went on to have a very high quality of life.

Research Efforts

During my professional career, I didn't have a lot of opportunities to do research. However, because of the large number of babies we cared for at the neonatal unit, we partnered with other academic centers in Florida doing clinical research.

One of the areas that provided me with satisfaction was my involvement with a national neonatal conference held in Orlando at one of the Disney World hotels. The event was titled, "The Management of the Tiny Baby Conference". The conference was launched in 1978 in association with the University of Florida Neonatal Division. I served as the chairman, moderator, and lecturer for 26 years. In that capacity, I met and interacted with the pioneers and individuals in the forefront of my specialty. Eventually, the conference achieved national recognition and was attended yearly by hundreds of individuals involved in the care of premature and critically ill infants. Shortly after I stepped down from my role as chairman, the conference was rebranded as the "Neo Conference" and is currently held in different locations around the country.

The Tiny Baby Initiative

The Tiny Baby Initiative was born through the success a few neonatal units were having in the saving and the improvement of life for at-risk premature babies. I was chosen with three of my colleagues based on our experiences and commitment to be part of this new program in our NICU. To get more information and guidance, I visited with one of our neonatal nurses and respiratory therapist Dr Jonathan Klein, a neonatologist in Iowa. For more than a decade, he and his team had been developing a comprehensive program with a group of doctors and nurses exclusively dedicated to the care of these tiny and critical babies. The improvement in survival and quality of life over more than a decade were impressive.

Tremendously impressed by these results, we returned to our facility and began this journey. Until the end of my career at the Winnie Palmer Hospital for Women and Babies neonatal unit, I was inspired and touched by the tenacity and will to survive these babies had, in spite of their size and multiple obstacles related to the immaturity of their organs and systems.

I was honored by the trust and belief their parents and families had in us. They were so appreciative of our efforts and the caring, commitment, and compassion we demonstrated during the care of their babies. The ties we developed with these babies and families were very deep and strong and have remained well after their discharge. They will stay permanently in our hearts and minds for the rest of our lives.

The Naming of the Neonatal Unit

It was the summer of 2010, exactly June 21st of that year, when the neonatal unit at Winnie Palmer Hospital for Women and Babies was named after me. I was recovering from two back surgeries for herniated discs at L2 and L3 and had very little appetite or energy. As a result, I lost 25 pounds.

My wife Adrienne and I received an invitation from the hospital foundation to attend an event at the Bay Hill Country Club to honor the medical staff of the newborn unit. I remember telling Annie that I didn't feel my best and perhaps we should stay home. After a few minutes of discussion back and forth, we decided to go. Upon our arrival, we were greeted by the members of the Orlando Health Foundation board as well as the CEOs of the Palmer Medical Center and the entire Orlando Health system. To my surprise, we were seated at the main table, and shortly after the program started, the president of the Orlando Health Board read a proclamation naming the newborn unit the Alexander Center for Neonatology.

I was totally in shock, and it took a few minutes for me to comprehend the magnitude of this honor. As I accepted and thanked my mother, wife, children, family, and staff for making this possible, a great sense of pride and fulfillment saturated my entire soul. For the next few years, I'll admit that it was a little bit eerie seeing my name at the entrance of the newborn unit where I still worked. I did my best to remain totally humble as just another member of the all-star team. Yet, I was so proud of this amazing honor. When new staff members were hired or new patients came in, I would tell them that the Alexander who was recognized on the building was an outstanding and dedicated doctor who built the unit, and I just happened to have the same last name.

Two years after I left, the name came down, but I was given the proclamation that is pictured in one of the pages of this book.

The End of One Road Leads to Another

I worked with at-risk babies for 42 years, seven months and nine days. That's 15,500 days in total. I left the neonatal unit and two hospitals that I helped to build, grow, and succeed. I still have dreams of caring for babies in this facility, and I wake up every morning with the sense that we made amazing strides in caring for premature and critical babies.

Since I left, I have received thousands of demonstrations of thanks and support from former patients, parents and relatives, physicians, staff, foundation members, and community leaders. I received so many texts, phone calls, e-mails, and Facebook messages on the Dr. Alexander, Kids and Families Facebook page. To my surprise, I also received an incredible book with close to 100 testimonials and thank you cards from nurses and respiratory therapists I worked with through the years. Many of those cards and testimonials are published throughout this book. These acts of kindness lift up my spirit and keep me grounded.

I think about the nearly 45,000 babies I helped care for, and I sincerely believe I will leave this world a better place because of my dedication to all of those tiny infants.

My soul and spirit remain intact and strong. Writing my autobiography is a way for me to move forward with my life in a positive way. I was born to be a doctor, and I am honored and proud of this gift God gave me. Based on my profound love, knowledge, and expertise, I will continue to deliver care through medical missions trips to underdeveloped countries with the hope of improving newborn care in these areas.

For those families and future generations, we impacted humanity, and in the process, this world is a better place. I practiced in the Golden Era of medicine where expert care, commitment, and compassion were the driving principles. There is still no better medical care than in the United States, and I'm proud that my generation of medical professionals raised the bar for others to rise to.

Chapter 15
Medical Mission Trips

Throughout their careers, many doctors utilize their skill set and experience to participate in medical mission trips. There are so many countries in the world that lack the resources and expertise that American doctors have, so sharing that wisdom is a wonderful experience for both the doctors and the patients and their families.

For me, during my career, I was so laser-focused on caring for large numbers of premature and critically ill babies and expanding the neonatal units in two hospitals, that medical missions never really entered my consciousness. I could have easily gone back to help people in Colombia but I was disconnected from that community. In fact, I only attended two medical school reunions in Colombia in 40 years.

Growing up in Colombia and experiencing poverty and hardship definitely instilled in me a great appreciation of the incredible medical facilities and expertise in the United States. Still, I didn't think about taking my show on the road, so to speak, until one day when I was giving a tour of our facility to a Colombian financial leader in Orlando. He was surprised to learn that I grew up in Colombia because my name doesn't reflect that and I look more European than South American. A few days after the tour, he introduced me to the president of Coamed, an organization of multi-specialist Colombian doctors practicing in Orlando. The extremely charismatic Dr Andres Perez, along with his wife Marta, led the organization and I quickly became involved. We planned medical missions trips to a couple of Colombia's Caribbean Islands in the San Andres y Providencia. We brought medical equipment, provided outpatient and odontologic services, as well as much-needed orthopedic surgeries. For my part, I secured some incubators, one transport incubator and supplies for newborn intensive care.

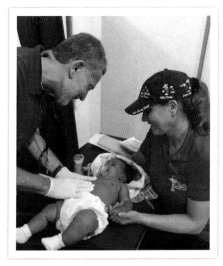

Dr. Aloxander on San Andres Island during a medical mission trip

While there, I toured the newborn unit with the neonatologist who was providing care and I was told during my second visit that the survival for this population improved exponentially as this population of babies received optimal temperature support from birth and afterwards.

During my last mission, in 2017, I brought my youngest son Gabriel, who was 12 at the time. Having been born and raised in the United States, the experience was a complete eye-opener for him, seeing how the rest of the world lives.

Since my departure from the Palmer Hospitals, I have continued to participate in other meaningful medical missions to the Dominican Republic with the Mission of Hope organization. In addition, I'm consulting via Zoom with a team of physicians from Saudi Arabia who are doing transports of critical babies to the capital city of Rijad.

Participating in medical missions has reinforced my belief that with the knowledge and the resources we have in this country we have the capability to impact the rest of the world. It has also given me the personal satisfaction to give back to the country where I was born, raised, and received my medical education.

As I finished my autobiography, I was hit with an unexpected health challenge and had to undergo open heart surgery to replace two abnormally functioning valves and reinforce my aorta artery. Thankfully, I am recovering quite well thanks to the gifted and caring cardiovascular surgeon Dr Kevin Accola and his team. I have been given the chance to continue pursuing my personal and professional dreams, which I'm sure will include more medical missions.

Chapter 16
My Extraordinary Family

I have been blessed with many miracles in my life, such as all of the wonderful people I've worked with and the thousands of incredible babies who struggled for their lives yet displayed an incomprehensible will to survive. And, of course, I've had a loving family around me, even with the ups and downs of marriage. Some of the most precious gifts are my four outstanding children and four grandchildren whom I love very deeply.

Of course, nothing is without challenges, and my oldest grandchild Alex has had his share. Alex was born at full-term gestation after an uncomplicated pregnancy and delivery from my daughter Lizette. All seemed to be going along perfectly. However, 12 hours after his birth, he developed generalized seizures and had a respiratory arrest requiring respiratory support. A former colleague of mine called me and described the events surrounding Alex's problems. I rushed to the hospital and to the radiology department to see how I could help. I was shocked to see the CT scan of his brain revealing major bleeding at the left hemisphere.

The irony was that I instantly became the grandfather of a NICU baby, providing emotional support to my daughter Lizette and son-in-law David and the rest of the family. This time, I was part of the family needing support. I always have shown empathy and caring toward my babies and families, but this experience with my grandson gave me even more insight and experience of what families go through. It made me a better person and a better doctor.

Dave, Alex, Lizette, and Emma Dunay

Josh, Jennifer, Alan, and Jordan Alexander (above)
David Alexander (right)

127

Alex's acute symptoms improved after a few days and he was discharged with anti-seizure medications and follow-up appointments with the pediatric neurologist and neurosurgeon. Soon, it became clear that Alex would have significant developmental challenges. Being a proactive mother, my daughter found out about some pioneers in the use of bone marrow and umbilical cord blood stem cells for the treatment of Alex's condition. Her research led to Monterrey, Mexico, where a pediatric hematologist was using infusions of baby's and children's bone marrow into their blood. Alex received these treatments, which resulted in modest motor improvement.

As the research in stem cells in the U.S. progressed, Lizette developed a non-profit foundation that financially supported this new and exciting genre of medicine. She subsequently moved to the National Board of Cerebral Palsy Alliance whose mission is the prevention and improvement in the quality of life for babies and children impacted by this and other conditions.

Alex's development was significantly affected by the bleeding in his brain (neonatal stroke), but he is truly a happy and loving person. We consider him to be a gift to our family and friends and to humanity. His treatment helped build a foundation to make a difference in present and future babies afflicted with this condition. It also heightened my understanding of the feelings families experience in these stressful situations.

I love my family unconditionally, yet there is a special love for Alex and the challenges he faces in life with a smile on his face and love in his heart.

My Wonderful Mother Manja

Dr. Alexander and his mother

The hardest part of moving away from Colombia was leaving my mother behind. Of course, she encouraged me to pursue my dreams in America, but I left a piece of my heart with her. I had been through a lot in my life and was still just 24 when I arrived in Detroit. Like any devoted son, I wrote letters to her every week and she did the same. Even though long distance telephone calls were expensive, I called her once a month just to hear her voice. We were in constant contact, but my goal was to get her to the United States.

> It took years of paperwork, phone calls, and red tape, but eventually, I was very fortunate to get my mother accepted to come to America. By that time, 16 years had passed. I had made my way to Orlando and had built a reputation of being a passionate and dedicated doctor. I was 38 years old and she was 75.

I was making enough money to buy her a condo close to my house so she could visit me and vice versa. Of all of my accomplishments in medicine, I'm maybe most proud that I was able to support her for the remainder of her life. No more 10-hour work days. No more toiling in the Canada Dry bottling factory. She could sleep late, eat whatever she wanted, go shopping, whatever. She could live a relaxing life and choose what she wanted to do. It was my small way of trying to give her back the love and support she had given to me and to repay her for the sacrifices she had made for me for me all my life.

A few years after she had been living in Orlando, she developed breast cancer. She was in her late 70s but was still a strong woman. Even though she had to have a unilateral mastectomy, she beat breast cancer without undergoing chemotherapy or radiation. Perhaps she'd been through so much that cancer was just another bump in the road for her. She continued living the good life for another decade when cancer returned in her colon when she was in her late 80s. One of my best friends and neighbor, a colorectal surgeon named Sergio Larach, removed the cancer and a portion of her colon and she fully recovered, celebrating her 90th birthday with family and friends.

> During her golden years, we talked by phone every day and I visited her often. I would tell her about the babies we were saving, and she was just amazed at what advanced medicine could accomplish. She told me stories about our family, and her mind remained as sharp as ever.

A few months after her 90th birthday, she had an episode of vomiting and diarrhea. When I saw her, she was frail, pale, and incoherent. I called an ambulance, and by the time she arrived at the hospital, she was in a coma. At the emergency room, we discovered that her cancer had recurred. I stayed by her bed in the hospital until midnight as she went in and out of her coma. When I left at midnight, she was comfortable and her vital signs were stable. I was planning to take her to her condo the next morning and get hospice care to help. However, at 4:45 a.m. my phone rang. In my gut, I knew that she had died. I felt so sad that I wasn't with her as she left this world, but I believe she wanted to protect me, as she always did, from the experience of her passing. She always watched over me, and this was her last act of kindness. Or so I thought.

A few months passed, and I thought about her every day. I was still extremely sad and somber and feeling guilty for leaving her that night. I was lying in bed getting ready to sleep, when all of a sudden, a circle of bright light appeared in front of me. In the center was my mother Manja, looking very young and happy. She was wearing a red blouse and a blue skirt and smiling. Slowly, she came toward me then kissed my left hand and disappeared. For at least an hour, I could barely move my left hand. It felt like a heavy weight was tied to it, but my heart was full of comfort and happiness knowing my mother had reached the ultimate celestial place and didn't want me to worry about her any more. Since that surreal experience, I have felt her presence every day of my life and I know she is always looking after me and will do so forever. To this day, I wear a neck chain with my mother's wedding ring hanging on it that she wore all her life.

Personal Life

While my professional life has been a series of amazing miracles, my personal life has had its share of ups and downs. First of all, I've been married a few times. That's about all I'm going to say about that.

> An amazing woman in my life was my dear mother Manja who instilled in me love and forgiveness. She inspired and supported me in my dreams and always believed in me. Her love confirmed in me the power of faith in God and the power of discipline and hard work.

My children: Lizette, Alan, Gabriel, and David, as well as my grandchildren, Alex, Emma, Jordan, and Josh, have had a tremendous impact on my soul and have made me a better person and doctor. Many thank-yous go to my wonderful sister Claudia, her husband Harold, and the rest of my German family, as well as my uncles, aunts, and cousins for all the love they have given me through the years.

There is also another amazing female friend who helped to shape my life. Sally, the office manager of our medical practice for 39 years, always showed unconditional love and support toward me. She became part of our family and was a friend to everybody connected to me.

I have deep love for my best friend Rap (Arthur Raptoulis), who has been like a brother for 45 years and became my counselor and a rock for me from a personal and professional point of view. I also have to thank and acknowledge my many friends who I have shared personal time with and who helped me to grow as a person. I have been blessed to have so many friends, too many in fact to try to name here.

I am also in debt to the many partners I've had over the years for their dedication to our profession and working every day to enrich the lives of our patients and their families, along with an amazing staff of more than 400 passionate professionals who saw the best in me and provided tremendous knowledge and caring in the pursuit of saving thousands of lives of the precious babies in our care.

Finally, I want to recognize my great friend and neighbor Sergio Larach for his unconditional friendship toward me and family for the last few decades.

My eternal gratitude to Arnold and Winnie Palmer for their support and belief that these two hospitals were needed and for lighting the torch for excellence in medical care for babies, children, and women everywhere.

To Amy (Palmer) and Roy Saunders for the unconditional support they have always given me and to their dedication to preserve the legacy of Amy's parents in making it possible for these two hospitals to become a reality of growth and success.

Dr. Alexander,

My family and I got to witness a beautiful miracle this year - Baby Alexander came home.

The challenges that he faced in the NICU were so great, but he made it through and we are eternally thankful.

The care that he received from the Doctors, Nurses and RT's, was exceptional. The care and special attention that he received from you was heart warming and it gave me and my husband great relief in a very difficult time.

When you told my eldest son that you wanted to save babies ever since you were a child, I understood just how blessed we were and I knew Alexander would come home. I was suppose to deliver in South Florida and ended up at WP, with you and your staff, a man who has dreamt of healing babies his entire life. In my mind, that meant my son is suppose to live. My faith was strong and your commitment was extraordinary. Thank you for saving me and my family! Thank you for saving my sweet baby.

Much love,
Megan Fletcher Garcia.

Chapter 17
Professional Awards

Dr. Alexander at the Walk for Winnie with a former patient and his mother

If you work in an industry for 42.5 years and do your job well, you will probably receive recognition for your accomplishments. Such was the case for me and my incredible team. I'm so proud of the success we had saving premature and critical care infants over all of those years. As a result, I was presented with many awards, but none of this would have been possible without the dedication and hard work of each and every person on our team.

Following are the meaningful awards received.

March 1983 - The Jefferson Award by the American Institute for Public Service

March 1986 - Recognition Award for Outstanding Achievement and Dedication to Health Care

April 1986 - The Spirit of Epcot Award by Walt Disney World Community Service

February 1997 - The Children's Charity Humanitarian award by Variety Club Organization

December 1998 - The Citizen of the Year Award by the March of Dimes for outstanding contributions to the medical profession, philanthropic leadership for the babies and families in Central Florida

March 2008 - The Children's Miracle Network Award for the care, support, and devotion to children

June 2011 - The Exemplary Physician Colleague Award by the Orlando Health System, nominated by neonatal nurses for compassion and caring and value of collaboration with staff

June 2011 - The Alexander Center for Neonatology, NICU named in my honor

September 2013 - Healing Hero Award for Excellence in Pediatric Medicine by the Kids Beating Cancer

November 2013 - Premio Médico Orgullo Colombiano by the Colombo American Association

December 2014 - The Don Quijote Award for Excellence by the Orlando Hispanic Chamber of Commerce

February 2020 - Special recognition service award from the City of Winter Park

Chapter 18

The Orchestral Gap
Between Heaven and Earth

By Gabriel Alexander

You mended velvet from silk,
Let those who could not live,
Live a life, fully built,

Silky stars,
I dream a dying dream,

Where fireballs reach as far
as eyes can see,
And cast the night with
blanket sheeth,

Letting those who weep,
have what they want and cling,

And so, by horse, by boat,
by exile, by holocaust,
Came a figure that defied
deaths will,
The weeping mother
was no more,

For now,
Her child could last the night,
For now,
One did not have to be
born into suffering,

Once we had cursed the night,
But now we could fight,

It is those who forfeit their
lives towards caring for the
lives of others,

That truly live,

We let the dying stars
make us sad,
But, they always cast the
brightest glows.

Dearest Greg -
     Some people are lucky & have the joy of having special people who are part of their lives - I have been blessed to have had extra special men in my life - my Paul, my beloved Dad & you!! Like a sponge - I - & all of us soaked up all that you taught us - but it went so much beyond the learning - it was the love & passion we felt caring for our patients & families. It is the NICU family we grew - together all these years!! A place we worked our tushies off for but always together & always knowing we could come to you anytime & any place. But you were always a part of some of the most important moments in Paul & my lives. Josh (I know - his was better because you did his!! LOL) & Adam's bris

& then their Bar Mitzvahs!! The boys grew up loving to visit the unit & say hi to Dr. A. I hope you will continue to share with us future simchas - since Josh & Kelly are having a girl - no bris but maybe a baby naming.
     I can't imagine you sitting still but I hope that you are able spend time with Annie, Gabriel & the rest of your family.
     I hope you feel all the love flowing to you from all of us because that love is forever dear friend!
     All our love - Paul, Josh, Adam, Shelby, Kelly & Maddy